Learning to Pass

New CLAiT

006

nit 2

ıksana Patel

w.heinemann.co.uk

ree online support
Jseful weblinks
4 hour online ordering

01865 888058

Heinemann

Inspiring generations

Heinemann Educational Publishers
Halley Court, Jordan Hill, Oxford OX2 8EJ
Part of Harcourt Education

Heinemann is the registered trademark of
Harcourt Education Limited

First published 2005

10 09 08 07 06 05
10 9 8 7 6 5 4 3 2 1

British Library Cataloguing in Publication Data is available
from the British Library on request.

10-digit ISBN: 0 43508260 4
13-digit ISBN: 978 0 43508260 4

Typeset by Thomson Digital, India

Original illustrations © Harcourt Education Limited, 2005

Cover design by Wooden Ark

Printed in the UK by Bath Colour

Cover photo: © Getty Images

Acknowledgements

The author would like to express her deep gratitude and appreciation to Abdul Patel for working
through the book several times and for his support, incredible patience and invaluable feedback
during the writing of this book. A special thank you to Fayaz and Fozia Roked for their help,
encouragement and support. Thank you to Elaine Tuffery, Lewis Birchon, Susan Ross and
Gavin Fidler.

Every effort has been made to contact copyright holders of material reproduced in this book. Any
omissions will be rectified in subsequent printings if notice is given to the publishers.

The publisher would like to thank Daydream Education (tel. 0800 068 0232
web. www.daydreameducation.co.uk) for kind permission to reproduce the image on page 14.

Microsoft product screenshots reprinted with permission from Microsoft Corporation.

Contents

An introduction to the qualification and a Definition of terms can be found on the CD-ROM that accompanies this book.

Who this book is suitable for

- *Anyone working towards:*
    - ✓ *OCR Level 1 Certification or Diploma for IT Users (New CLAiT)*
    - ✓ *OCR ITQ qualification*
- *Complete beginners as no prior knowledge of Excel is required.*
- *Use as a self-study workbook – the user should work through the book from start to finish.*
- *Tutor-assisted workshops or tutor-led groups.*
- *Any individual wanting to learn to use Microsoft Office Excel 2003*

Although this book is based on Excel 2003, it is also suitable for users of Excel 2002 (XP) and Excel 2000. Note that a few of the skills may be slightly different and some screenshots will not be identical.

UNIT 2: Creating spreadsheets and graphs

For the first part of Unit 2, you will need to create a spreadsheet, use basic formulae and functions, and edit a spreadsheet.

You will use a software program called Microsoft Office Excel 2003, which is part of Microsoft Office 2003. Excel will help you to create spreadsheets and perform calculations on numbers quickly and easily. We will refer to it as Excel from now on. Default settings are assumed.

This chapter is divided into two sections:

○ *in Section 1 you will learn how to create a new spreadsheet, use basic formulae and basic functions, and save and print a spreadsheet*

○ *in Section 2 you will learn how to edit and format spreadsheets, and display and print formulae.*

How to work through this chapter

1 Before you begin this unit, make sure that you feel confident with the basics of using a computer and Windows XP. These skills are covered in Chapter 1 of the Unit 1 book *Learning to Pass New CLAiT: File management and e-document production.*

2 Read the explanation of a term first.

3 If there are terms that you do not understand, refer to the Definition of terms on the CD-ROM.

4 Work through the book in sequence so that one skill is understood before moving on to the next. This ensures thorough understanding of the topic and prevents unnecessary mistakes.

5 Read the ▶▶ *How to...* guidelines which give step-by-step instructions for each skill; do not attempt to work through them. Read through each point and look at the screenshots – make sure that you understand all the instructions before moving on.

6 To make sure that you have understood how to perform a skill, work through the **Check your understanding** task that follows. You should refer to the **How to...** guidelines when doing the task.

7 At the end of each section is an **Assess your skills** table. This lists the skills that you will have practised by working through each section.

Look at each item listed to help you decide whether you are confident that you can perform each skill.

8   At the end of the the book there are **Quick reference guides**, **Build-up** and **Practice tasks**. Work through each of the tasks.

If you need help, you may refer to the How to... guidelines or Quick reference guides whilst doing the Build-up tasks. Whilst working on the Practice task, you should feel confident enough to use only the Quick reference guides if you need support. These guides may also be used during an assessment.

A CD-ROM accompanies this book. Solutions for the spreadsheet tasks can be found in the folder **ss_worked_copies**.

Preparing your work area

It is advisable to prepare your user area to keep your files organised.

An example of a folder structure for all units is shown in Figure 2.1 below. The main folder in **My Documents** is called **Ruks Clait 2006 Level 1**. Within this folder are subfolders for each of the units.

You may not need to create as many folders or you may prefer to create a folder for a unit when you begin a new unit or a new chapter.

For Unit 2, two subfolders have been created, one for Spreadsheets and another for Graphs (Figure 2.1).

TIP!

There are many ways of performing the skills covered in this book. This book provides **How to...** guidelines that have proven to be easily understood by learners.

What does it mean?

User area
A user area is the workspace on a computer where you will save your files. One example of a user area is a folder called **My Documents**; Windows XP creates this area. In a centre, you may be given a work area on a network. This area may have a drive name, e.g. G drive. Alternatively, you may save your work on a floppy disk, which is usually the A drive. On your own personal computer, your user area may be the C drive.

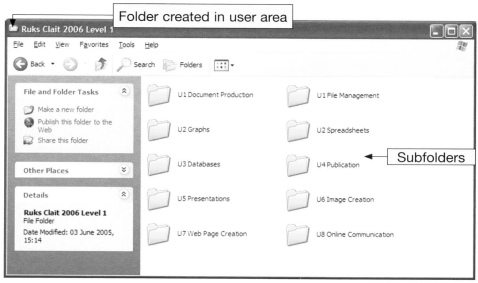

FIGURE 2.1 Folders in the user area

Within each unit subfolder, there are further subfolders.

For example, in the **U2 Spreadsheets** subfolder, the two subfolders are:

1 **U2 Chap 1 Ssheets working** – this is the working folder in which all files will be saved.

2 **ss_worked_copies** – this folder has been copied from the CD-ROM.

These subfolders are shown in Figure 2.2.

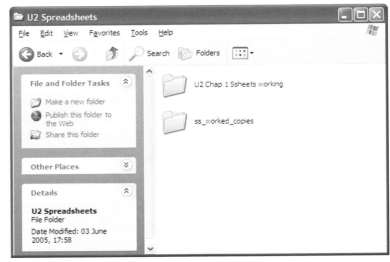

FIGURE 2.2 Subfolders in the **U2 Spreadsheets** subfolder

1: Create a new spreadsheet

LEARNING OUTCOMES

In this section you will learn how to:

- start Excel
- identify the different parts of Excel
- enter data into a spreadsheet
- widen columns to display the data in full
- set page layout (margins, orientation)
- save a spreadsheet into a new folder
- insert text in headers and footers
- insert automatic date and filename in headers and footers
- save an updated spreadsheet
- close a spreadsheet
- understand the difference between formulae and functions
- use mathematical operators * / - + in formulae
- replicate (copy) formulae and functions
- use basic functions (sum, average)
- use brackets in formulae
- use Print Preview
- print spreadsheet data.

What is a spreadsheet?

A spreadsheet is used to manipulate figures, a spreadsheet program is one created specifically to help process tabular information, usually numbers. Any task involving the use of numbers can be done on a spreadsheet. The advantage of a spreadsheet over other methods of manipulating data (e.g. tables in Microsoft Word) is its ability to constantly update (recalculate) figures automatically. Once a spreadsheet has been set up correctly, its calculations will always be correct and any changes to data will recalculate automatically.

Spreadsheet terms and actions will be explained throughout this chapter.

Mouse techniques

Unless otherwise instructed, always click using the **left** mouse button.

MOUSE ACTION	DESCRIPTION
Point	Move the mouse on the mousemat until the pointer appears at the required position on the screen.
Click	Press and release the **left** mouse button once.
Double-click	Quickly press the left mouse button **twice**, then release it.
Right-click	Press the **right** mouse button once – a menu displays.
Hover	Position the mouse pointer over an icon or menu item and pause, a **Tool tip** or a further menu item will appear.
Click and drag	Used to move items. Click with the left mouse button on any item, hold the mouse button down and move the pointer to another location. Release the mouse button.

Mouse techniques

Switch on your computer and log in.

Starting Excel

▶▶ How to...   *Start Excel*

1   On the desktop, click on **Start**.

2   From the **Windows XP Start** menu, click on **All Programs**.

3 From the **All Programs** menu, click on **Microsoft Office** (Figure 2.3).

4 From the list of Microsoft Office programs, click on **Microsoft Office Excel 2003**.

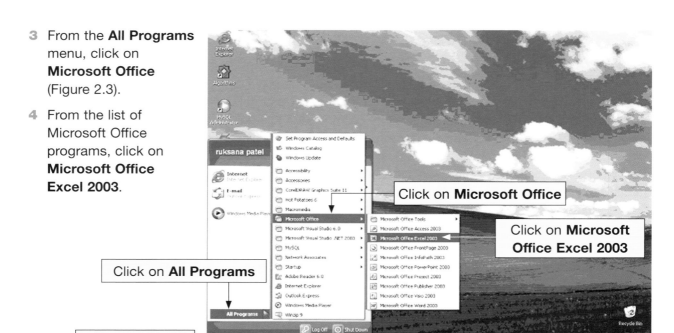

Click on **Microsoft Office**

Click on **Microsoft Office Excel 2003**

Click on **All Programs**

Click on **Start**

FIGURE 2.3 Starting Microsoft Office Excel 2003

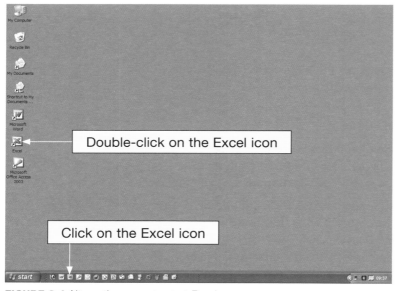

Double-click on the Excel icon

Click on the Excel icon

FIGURE 2.4 Alternative ways to start Excel

Check your understanding *Start Excel*

1 Start Excel, either through the **Start** menu or by using a shortcut icon.

2 A new blank workbook called **Book1** is displayed.

3 Keep this spreadsheet file open.

Getting familiar with the Excel window

Excel 2003 may open with the **task pane** on the right. Click on the black cross to close the task pane (Figure 2.5).

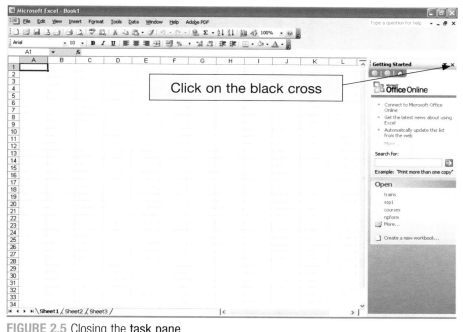

Click on the black cross

FIGURE 2.5 Closing the **task pane**

Now take a few minutes to learn about the different parts of the Excel window (Figure 2.6).

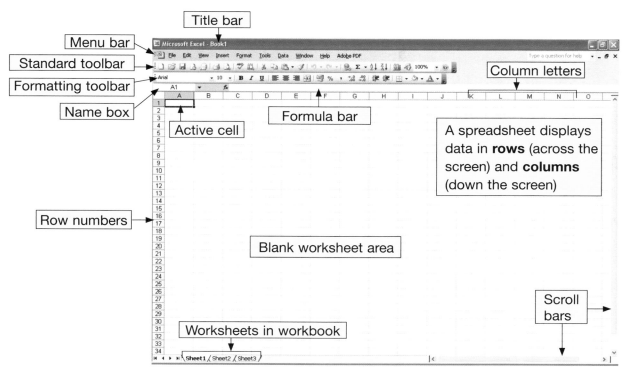

Title bar

Menu bar

Standard toolbar

Formatting toolbar

Name box

Active cell

Formula bar

Column letters

A spreadsheet displays data in **rows** (across the screen) and **columns** (down the screen)

Row numbers

Blank worksheet area

Scroll bars

Worksheets in workbook

FIGURE 2.6 The Excel window

PART OF WINDOW	DESCRIPTION
Title bar	Displays the title of the current workbook (spreadsheet file).
Menu bar	A list of options, click on a menu item to see the drop-down menu.
Standard toolbar	Includes icons for commonly used tasks, e.g. save, print.
Formatting toolbar	Includes icons for commonly used formatting, e.g. bold, centre.
Blank workbook	The main window made up of cells where data and formulae are entered.
Cell	At the point where a row and column cross, a cell is formed. The cell that the user clicks in is known as the active cell (has a thick outline around it). A cell may contain text, numbers or formula.
Cell reference	Each cell has a unique cell address made up of the column letter and the row number (e.g. **A1**), this is displayed in the **Name box**.
Formula bar	Displays data or formulae being entered in a cell. When a cell is clicked, the full contents or the formula used are displayed here.
Name box	Displays the active cell reference. A cell can also be given a specific name.
Columns	Identified by letters, known as column headings. Columns go down a spreadsheet.
Rows	Identified by numbers, known as row headings. Rows go across a spreadsheet.
Workbook	A spreadsheet file – a workbook usually contains more than one worksheet.
Worksheet	Excel term for a spreadsheet – the tabs at the bottom of the screen show the number of worksheets included in a spreadsheet file (workbook).
Status bar	Displays the status of the current spreadsheet.
Scroll bar	Allows you to scroll up/down or left/right to view your spreadsheet.

The Excel window

Getting familiar with Excel

If the **Office Assistant** icon is visible in an Excel spreadsheet, right-click on it. From the menu displayed, click on **Hide** to remove the Office Assistant from the screen.

1 In your spreadsheet, look for the **Menu bar** (Figure 2.7).

2 Click on **Edit** to display the **Edit** menu. At first, the whole menu may not display, but if you leave it open for a few seconds it displays in full (Figure 2.8).

3 Another way to display the full menu is to click on the chevrons ⌄ button at the bottom of the menu as soon as the menu drops down.

4 Click on the **Edit** menu to close it.

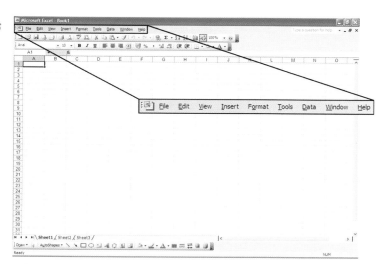

FIGURE 2.7 The **Menu bar**

The toolbar buttons

In your spreadsheet, move the mouse over each **toolbar** button and pause, a **Tool tip** displays showing the name of the button. In this book, we will refer to a toolbar button as an **icon**.

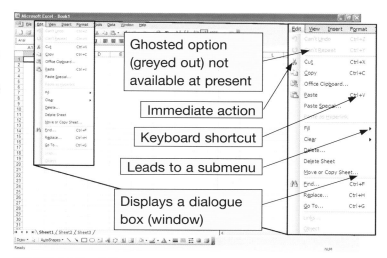

Ghosted option (greyed out) not available at present

Immediate action

Keyboard shortcut

Leads to a submenu

Displays a dialogue box (window)

FIGURE 2.8 The **Edit** menu

Making the Excel window clearer

The task pane

Excel 2003 opens with the **task pane** on the right of the screen (Figure 2.9). It is advisable to close the **task pane** so that the screen is clearer (optional).

Either click on the black cross just above the **task pane** to close it every time you start Excel, or set the option to close the **task pane** so that it does not display every time you start Excel.

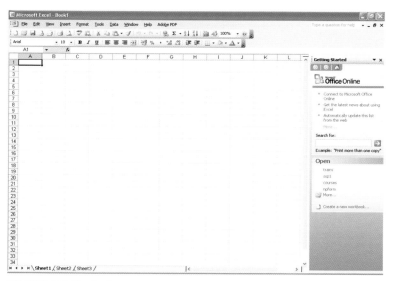

FIGURE 2.9 The **task pane**

 **How to...** *set the option to close the task pane (optional)*

1 In Excel, click on **Tools** (Figure 2.10).

2 From the **Tools** menu, click on **Options**.

3 The **Options** dialogue box is displayed.

4 Click on the **View** tab to select it (Figure 2.11).

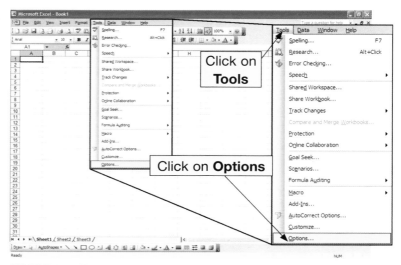

FIGURE 2.10 The Tools menu

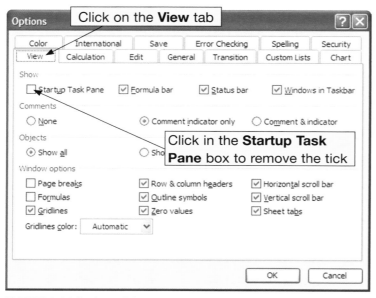

FIGURE 2.11 Options dialogue box with View tab selected

5 Click in the **Startup Task Pane** box to remove the tick.

6 Click on **OK**.

7 The **task pane** will no longer display every time you start Excel.

Standard and Formatting toolbars

Look at your spreadsheet. Are the **Standard** and **Formatting toolbars** on the same row as shown in Figure 2.12.

FIGURE 2.12 Standard and Formatting toolbars on the same row

If so, it is helpful to display them on two rows so that you can see all the icons on both toolbars.

▶▶ How to... *display the standard and formatting toolbars on two rows (optional)*

1 In your spreadsheet, click on the **Toolbar Options** symbol at the right end of the **Standard toolbar**.

2 A menu is displayed (Figure 2.13).

3 Click on **Show Buttons on Two Rows**.

4 The **Standard** and **Formatting toolbars** will now display on two rows (Figure 2.14).

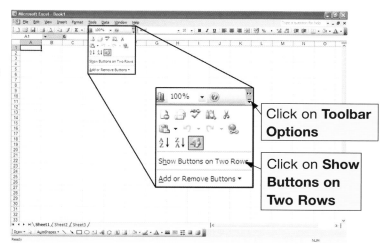

Click on **Toolbar Options**

Click on **Show Buttons on Two Rows**

FIGURE 2.13 More buttons menu

FIGURE 2.14 Standard and Formatting toolbars on separate rows

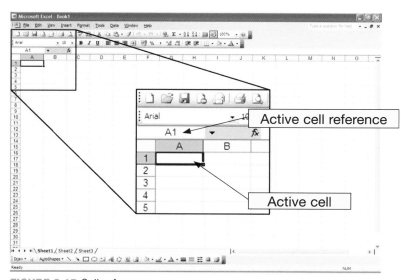

Active cell reference

Active cell

FIGURE 2.15 Cell reference

What does it mean?

Cell reference
When a cell is clicked, the cell reference is displayed in the **Name box**. This will be the column letter followed by the row number, e.g. **A1** is the active cell in the spreadsheet in Figure 2.15.

Moving around a spreadsheet

You can move from cell to cell using the cursor keys (arrow keys) on the keyboard (Figure 2.16).

FIGURE 2.16 The cursor keys

KEY	ACTION
↑ Up arrow key	Moves to the cell above the active cell.
↓ Down arrow key	Moves to the cell below the active cell.
← Left arrow key	Moves to the cell left of the active cell.
→ Right arrow key	Moves to the cell right of the active cell.

Using the cursor keys

▶▶ **How to...** *highlight cells in a spreadsheet*

HIGHLIGHT	METHOD
Cells that are next to each other	*Method 1:* Click with the mouse in the first cell. On the keyboard, hold down the **Shift** key. Click in the last cell. *Method 2:* Click in the first cell, when the white cross displays, drag the mouse across the range (block) of cells to be highlighted.
One column	Place the mouse pointer on a grey column letter and click.
One row	Place the mouse pointer on a grey row number and click.
Entire spreadsheet	*Method 1:* Click in the first cell and drag the mouse across to the last cell. *Quick method:* Click on the grey shaded cell to the left of the column letter **A** and above the row number **1** (Figure 2.17).

Highlighting cells

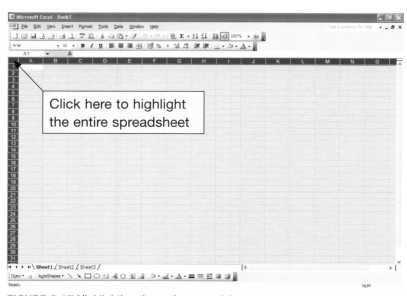

Click here to highlight the entire spreadsheet

FIGURE 2.17 Highlighting the entire spreadsheet

1 In your spreadsheet file **Book1**, look for the active cell (shown by a dark border). It should be **A1**, if not, click in **A1**.

2 Use the cursor keys to move:

a down to cell **A4**

b then to the right to cell **C4**

c then up to cell **C1**

d then to the left to cell **B1**.

3 Refer to the Highlighting cells table on page 12 and highlight cells as follows:

a from cell **B1** to **H1**

b column **C**

c row **5**

d the entire spreadsheet.

4 Practise moving around your spreadsheet until you feel confident.

Entering data

Numbers can be entered using the **Number keypad** on the right of the keyboard (check that the **Num Lock** key is switched on), or by using the number keys above the letters (Figure 2.18).

You must enter numbers in a spreadsheet with 100 per cent accuracy. One incorrect number can give incorrect information and will lead to all calculations using that number being incorrect.

When you enter text, make sure you **enter the words exactly** as shown.

Use the **same case** as shown in the text you are copying:

○ *this text is in **lower case** – there are no capital letters*

○ *Each Of These Words Has An **Initial Capital** – The First Letter Of Each Word Is A Capital*

○ *THIS TEXT IS IN **UPPER CASE** – ALL THE LETTERS ARE CAPITAL LETTERS.*

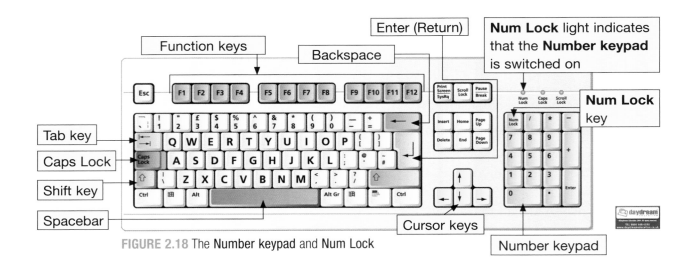

FIGURE 2.18 The **Number keypad** and Num Lock

▶▶ **How to...** *enter text and numbers*

HOW TO...	ACTION
Type one capital letter	Hold down the **Shift** key and press the required letter on the keyboard, then let go of the **Shift** key.
Type word(s) in capital letters	Press down the **Caps Lock** to switch it on (a light may indicate that **Caps Lock** is on).
Type lower case letters	Check the **Caps Lock** is switched off. If not press down the **Caps Lock** key to turn it off.
Insert a space between words	Press the **spacebar** once.
Delete a letter to the left of the cursor in an active cell	Press the **Backspace** key.
Enter numbers	Use the number keys above the QWERTY keys or press **Num Lock** and use the **Number keypad** (a light may indicate that **Num Lock** is on).
Enter a decimal point	Use the full stop key on the keyboard or the **decimal point** key on the **Number keypad**.

Using the keyboard

In Excel, data is entered into the active cell. Cells can contain:

- *text (labels)*
- *numbers (values)*
- *formulae (calculations).*

To make a cell active, ready to enter data or formula into it, either click in the cell, or use the cursor keys to move to the cell.

When data is being entered into a cell, that data also appears in the **Formula bar**.

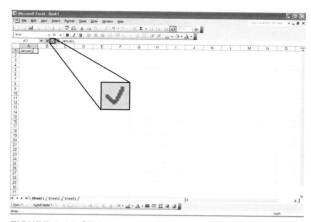

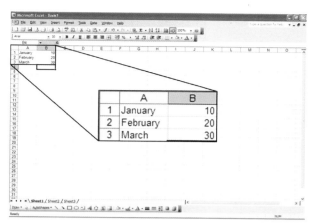

FIGURE 2.19 Clicking on the Enter tick in the Formula bar enters the data

FIGURE 2.20 Text is automatically left-aligned, numbers are right-aligned

To finish entering data into a cell, either:

○ press **Enter**

○ click with your mouse in another cell

○ use the cursor keys to move to another cell, or

○ click on the **Enter** tick in the **Formula bar** (Figure 2.19).

In Excel, when text is entered it is automatically left-aligned in the cell (placed to the left of the cell). Numbers are automatically right-aligned (placed to the right of the cell) (Figure 2.20).

Column labels

These are titles that identify the data in a column and are usually text. Column labels are sometimes referred to as column headings, but column headings are actually the grey column letters, **A**, **B**, **C**, etc.

Row labels

These are usually text and are generally entered in column **A**. Row labels are titles that identify the data in a row. Row numbers are the grey numbers **1**, **2**, **3**, etc. on the left of the screen.

▶▶ How to... enter data

1 In your spreadsheet, click in the cell where you want to enter data.

2 Enter the data.

3 Move to the next cell.

4 Enter the required data in the new cell.

TIP!

When you enter a long column heading or a row label, do not worry if the words extend into the second column. Columns can be widened later.

5 Move to the next cell.

6 Enter the rest of the data into the spreadsheet by moving from cell to cell.

7 Check all data is entered in the correct cell and that numbers are entered with 100 per cent accuracy.

1 In your spreadsheet file **Book1**, enter the text in column **A** as shown in Figure 2.21. Leave a blank cell in row **2**.

2 The text will not fit into the cells in column **A**. Some of the text will stretch across column **2**. This is normal – you will learn to widen columns later.

3 Keep the file **Book1** open.

	A	B	C
1	Popular Tourist Attractions		
2			
3	Chicago		
4	Great Barrier Reef		
5	Victoria Falls		
6	Niagara Falls		
7	Dubai		
8			

FIGURE 2.21 Text to be entered in **Book1**

Widening columns

When data is entered into an active cell in a spreadsheet, it may not fit in the cell. If the adjacent cell(s) are blank, the data is fully displayed, but if there is data in the adjacent cell(s), the data remains in the cell, but is not fully displayed. This is referred to as **truncated data**.

If cell(s) containing numbers are not wide enough, the data appears as ##### (hash signs). Once the cells are widened, the numbers will display.

Cells may be widened before or after data is entered in order to display data in full.

▶▶ How to... *widen columns*

1 Position the mouse pointer within the grey column letters over the vertical line to the right of the column to be widened.

2 The mouse pointer changes into ↔.

3 Double-click with the left mouse button.

4 Excel automatically adjusts the column width to display data in full.

5 Another method is to drag ↔ to make the column wider until all data is displayed in full.

TIP!

To adjust all columns after data has been entered, use **AutoFit**. Highlight the entire spreadsheet and double-click in the grey area between any two columns to display data in full in all columns.

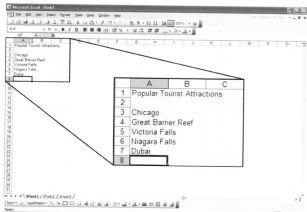

FIGURE 2.22 Column **A** when data is first entered

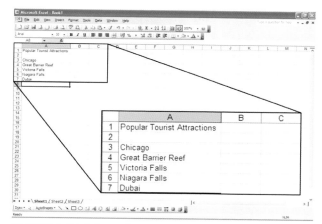

FIGURE 2.23 Column **A** after widening column

Check your understanding
Widen columns and enter more text and numbers

1 In your file **Book 1**, make column A wider so that all data is displayed in full.

2 Enter the data into column **B** as shown in Figure 2.24.

3 Keep the file **Book1** open.

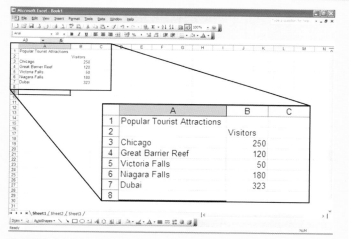

FIGURE 2.24 Data to be entered into column B

Page orientation

What does it mean?

Page orientation
Page orientation refers to which way round the paper is displayed:
Portrait – an A4 sheet of paper displayed with the shortest sides at the top and bottom.
Landscape – an A4 sheet displayed with the longest sides at the top and bottom.

> ▶▶ **How to...** set the page orientation

1 In the **Menu bar**, click on **File**.

2 From the **File** menu, click on **Page Setup**.

3 The **Page Setup** dialogue box is displayed (Figure 2.25).

4 Select the **Page** tab.

5 Click on **Portrait** or **Landscape**.

6 Click on **OK**.

7 The page will either be displayed portrait or landscape.

Margins

In Excel, you can set the top, bottom, left and right margins.

▶▶ How to...   *set margins*

1 In the **Menu bar**, click on **File**.

2 From the **File** menu, click on **Page Setup**.

3 The **Page Setup** dialogue box is displayed.

4 Click on the **Margins** tab to select it (Figure 2.26).

5 Click in the box for **Top**, enter the measurements for the top margin, then do the same for the **Left**, **Right** and **Bottom** margins (Figure 2.26).

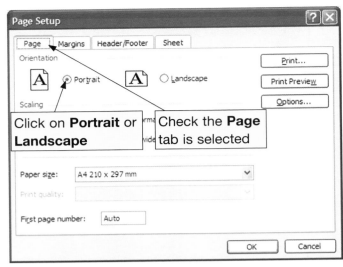

FIGURE 2.25 Page Setup dialogue box

What does it mean?

Margins
Margins are the amount of white space from the edge of the paper to the text on the page.

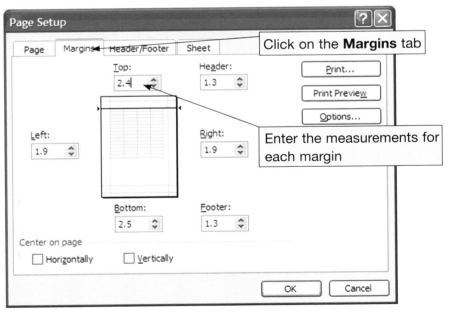

FIGURE 2.26 Setting the margins

6 You can use the **up/down arrows**, however, this may not allow you to set margins to specific measurements.

7 Click on **OK** to set the margins.

1 In your file **Book 1**, set the page orientation to **portrait**.

2 Set the top, bottom, left and right margins to **2.4 cm**.

3 Keep the file **Book1** open.

TIP!

Press the **Tab** key to move from one margin box to the next.

Saving a spreadsheet

It is good practice to save your work approximately every 10 minutes so that you do not lose too much work if there is a computer problem. Whenever you save a file, you should save it in your own user area.

TIP!

Save your files inside folders to keep your files organised, instead of saving all files into one user area.

▶▶ How to... *save a spreadsheet into a new folder from within Excel*

1 In the **Menu bar**, click on **File**.

2 From the **File** menu, click on **Save As**.

3 The **Save As** dialogue box is displayed.

4 Click on the **down arrow** to the right of the **Save in** box.

5 A list of user areas is displayed.

6 Click on your user area, then double-click on any folders to open the required subfolder.

7 The folder name displays in the **Save in** box

8 Click on the **Create New Folder** icon (Figure 2.27).

9 A **New Folder** dialogue box appears (Figure 2.28).

10 Enter the new folder name.

11 Click on **OK** to create a new folder.

12 In the **Save As** dialogue box, in the **File name** box, delete any existing text.

13 Enter the required filename.

14 In the **Save as type** box, check **Microsoft Excel Workbook** is displayed.

15 Click on **Save**.

16 Your spreadsheet will be saved in a new folder within your user area.

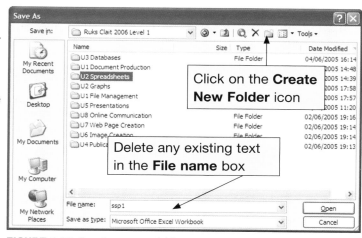

Click on the **Create New Folder** icon

Delete any existing text in the **File name** box

FIGURE 2.27 Creating a new folder

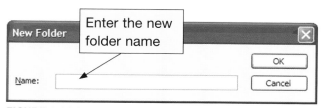

Enter the new folder name

FIGURE 2.28 New Folder dialogue box

Check your understanding Save your spreadsheet

1 Save your file **Book1** using the filename **ssp1** into a new folder called **ssheets** in your user area.

2 Keep the file **ssp1** open.

Headers and footers

Any text entered into the header or footer of a spreadsheet will appear on every print of the same worksheet and will also appear in the header or footer if the spreadsheet is saved with a different filename. In Excel, unlike headers and footers in Word, there are three sections in the header and footer dialogue box.

What does it mean?

Headers and footers
- A header is the space within the top margin.
- A footer is the space within the bottom margin.

How to... *add a header or footer*

1 In the **Menu bar**, click on **View**.

2 From the **View** menu, click on **Header and Footer**.

3 A **Page Setup** dialogue box is displayed (Figure 2.29).

4 Check the **Header/Footer** tab is selected.

5 Click on the **Custom Header** button.

6 A **Header** dialogue box opens (Figure 2.30).

7 Click in the **Left**, **Center** or **Right section**.

8 Enter the required information in the header.

9 Click on **OK** to close the **Header** dialogue box.

10 In the **Page Setup** dialogue box, click on the **Custom Footer** button.

11 A **Footer** dialogue box opens.

12 Click in the **Left**, **Center** or **Right section**.

13 Enter the required information in the footer.

14 Click on **OK** to close the **Footer** dialogue box.

15 Click on **OK** to close the **Page Setup** dialogue box.

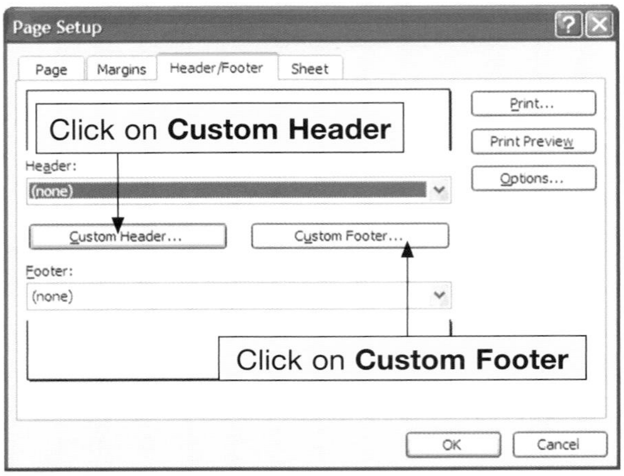

FIGURE 2.29 Page Setup dialogue box

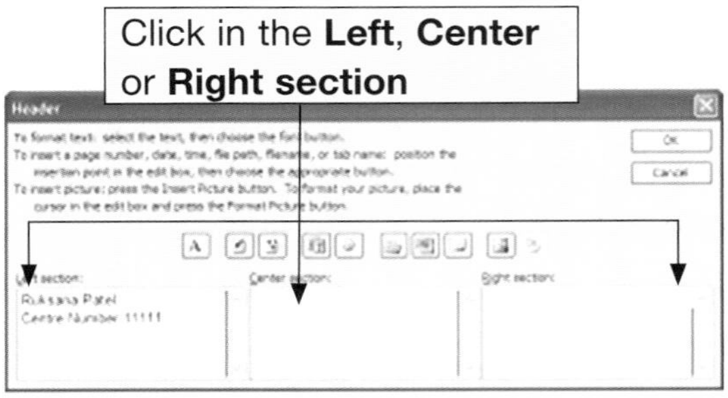

FIGURE 2.30 Header dialogue box

TIP!

The cursor is left aligned in the **Left section**, centred in the **Center section**, and right-aligned in the **Right section**.

Automatic fields

Excel can insert some information automatically into headers and footers, e.g. automatic dates and automatic filenames. The advantage of using automatic fields is that these will update automatically.

1 In the **Menu bar**, click on **View**.

2 From the **View** menu, click on **Header and Footer**.

3 Check the **Header/Footer** tab is selected.

4 Click on the **Custom Header** or **Custom Footer** button.

5 In the **Header** or **Footer** dialogue box, click in the **Left**, **Center** or **Right section** (Figure 2.31).

Click on the **Automatic Date** icon

Click on the **Automatic Filename** icon

An automatic filename is inserted in the **Left section**

An automatic date is inserted in the **Center section**

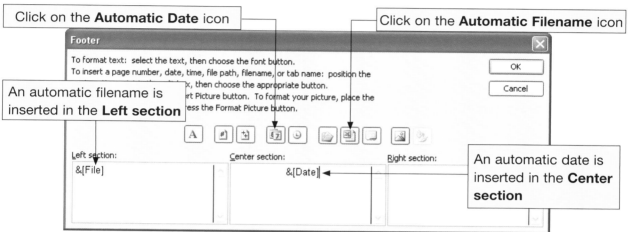

FIGURE 2.31 Footer dialogue box

6 Click on the icon to insert an automatic date. **&[Date]** is displayed in the selected section.

7 Click on the icon to insert an automatic filename. **&[File]** is displayed in the selected section.

8 Click on **OK** to confirm the header or footer.

9 Click on **OK** to close the **Page Setup** dialogue box.

Remember to save your document again after you have added headers and footers.

Saving and closing an existing spreadsheet

▶▶ How to... *save an existing spreadsheet*

1 In the **Menu bar**, click on **File**.

2 From the **File menu**, click on **Save** to save the spreadsheet.

▶▶ How to... *close a spreadsheet*

1 In the **Menu bar**, click on **File**.

TIP!

In the **Header** or **Footer** window, the automatic fields do not display the actual date, filename, etc. Click on the [Print Preview] button in the **Page Setup** dialogue box to view the headers and footers. The correct automatic headers and footers will display.

TIP!

You can also preview your spreadsheet by clicking on the **Print Preview** icon on the **Standard toolbar**.

TIP!

Alternatively click on the Save icon.

2 From the **File menu**, click on **Close** to close the spreadsheet (Figure 2.32).

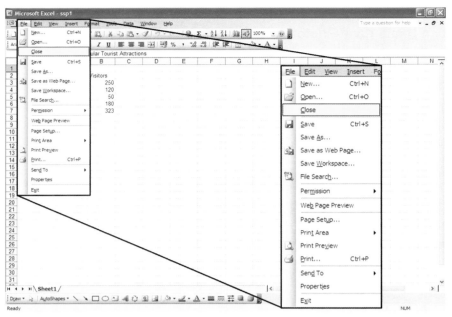

FIGURE 2.32 Click on **Close** in the **File** menu

Check your understanding
Add headers and footers including automatic fields

1 In your file **ssp1**, add the following headers and footers.

  a In the header, add your **first and last name** in the **Left section**.

  b In the header add your **centre number** in the **Center section**.

  c In the footer, insert an **automatic date** and an **automatic filename** in the **Left section**.

2 Save your spreadsheet keeping the filename **ssp1**.

3 Close your spreadsheet.

Why are formulae and functions used in spreadsheets?

In Excel, a calculation is called a **formula** (plural **formulae**) or a **function**.

Formulae

The advantage of using a formula is that when a number is changed, all calculations using that number are automatically recalculated.

Formulae are instructions to the program to perform calculations. Formulae are used to multiply, divide, add and subtract numbers in a spreadsheet.

A formula consists of:

- the **equals (=) sign**
- the **first cell reference**
- the **mathematical operator**
- the **second cell reference**.

Example of a simple formula: **=B3+C3**

A formula may also contain brackets, more than one mathematical operator and numbers instead of cell references.

What does it mean?

Mathematical operators
The mathematical operators are:
*
/
+
-

Functions

Functions are specialised formulae that make calculations easier. They are instructions to the program to carry out a particular process, and as such are pre-programmed formulae that carry out specific operations. Each function has a word that Excel recognises as an instruction, e.g. **SUM**, **AVERAGE**. The advantage of using a function is that it performs a multi-stage calculation in one step.

Functions consist of three parts:

- the **equals (=) sign**
- the **function name**
- the **range of cells**.

Example of a function: **=SUM(B3:H3)**

SUM and **AVERAGE** are two frequently used functions.

FUNCTION	CALCULATION	DISPLAYED AS	WHAT THE FUNCTION DOES
SUM	Adds all the numbers in a range of cells.	**=SUM(B3:F3)**	Adds all the cells starting from **B3** and ending at **F3**, i.e. adds **B3**, **C3**, **D3**, **E3**, **F3**.
AVERAGE	Calculates the average value of a range of cells.	**=AVERAGE(B3:B7)**	Adds all the cells starting at **B3** and ending at **B7**, then divides this figure by the number of cells in this range, i.e. adds **B3**, **B4**, **B5**, **B6**, **B7**, then divides the total by **5**.

The SUM and AVERAGE functions

The difference between formulae and functions

Look at the spreadsheet in Figure 2.33. To calculate the **Total Course Fee** for **Word Processing**, the numbers for **Jan**, **Feb**, **Mar**, **Apr**, **Jun** need to be added.

The calculation can be carried out using either a formula or a function. Both methods would give the correct result of **94**.

The **function** would be **=SUM(B3:F3)** The **formula** would be **=B3+C3+D3+E3+F3**

	A	B	C	D	E	F	G
1	Course Fees						
2		Jan	Feb	Mar	Apr	Jun	Total Course Fee
3	Word Processing	20	18	22	15	19	94
4	Spreadsheets	22	20	24	18	22	106
5	Databases	24	21	26	17	22	110
6	Web Pages	28	25	29	22	26	130
7	Desktop Publishing	28	26	26	24	28	132

FIGURE 2.33 Performing the calculation using either a formula or a function gives the same result at this stage

You may have noticed that there is no column data for **May!** If the **May** column data were to be inserted between **Apr** and **Jun**, the **function** would automatically update to:

=SUM(B3:G3)

and the new **Total Course Fee** would be automatically recalculated (Figure 2.34).

	A	B	C	D	E	F	G	H	I
1	Course Fees								
2		Jan	Feb	Mar	Apr	May	June	Total Course Fee	
3	Word Processing	20	18	22	15	17	19	111	
4	Spreadsheets	22	20	24	18	19	22	125	
5	Databases	24	21	26	17	16	22	126	
6	Web Pages	28	25	29	22	21	26	151	
7	Desktop Publishing	28	26	30	24	23	28	159	
8									

FIGURE 2.34 Where a function is used, the Total Course Fee is automatically recalculated when the **May** column data is added

However, the **formula** would remain the same and so would the result, which would now be incorrect, as it does not include the figures for **May**

(Figure 2.35). The user would have to remember to change the formula to:
=B3+C3+D3+E3+F3+G3.

	A	B	C	D	E	F	G	H	I
1	Course Fees								
2		Jan	Feb	Mar	Apr	May	June	Total Course Fee	
3	Word Processing	20	18	22	15	17	19	94	
4	Spreadsheets	22	20	24	18	19	22	106	
5	Databases	24	21	26	17	16	22	110	
6	Web Pages	28	25	29	22	21	26	130	
7	Desktop Publishing	28	26	30	24	23	28	136	
8									

FIGURE 2.35 Where a formula is used, the formula does not automatically recalculate, the **Total Course Fee** is now incorrect because it does not include the **May** data

In this example a function is a more appropriate choice than a formula.

Mathematical operators

Look for the **mathematical operators** on your keyboard. The symbols can be found either on the **Number keypad** or on the main part of the keyboard.

MATHEMATICAL FUNCTION	KEYBOARD SYMBOL	KEYBOARD KEY
Multiply	*	**Shift** key and number **8**
Divide	/	**/** key next to the full stop
Add	+	**Shift** key and **=** key
Subtract	-	**-** key above the **P**

Mathematical functions

▶▶ How to... *create a simple formula using a mathematical operator*

1 In your spreadsheet, click in the cell in which the formula is to be created.

2 Enter the = sign.

3 The = sign displays in the **Formula bar** and in the active cell (Figure 2.36).

TIP!

When **=** is entered in a cell, Excel knows that a calculation is going to be created in that cell.

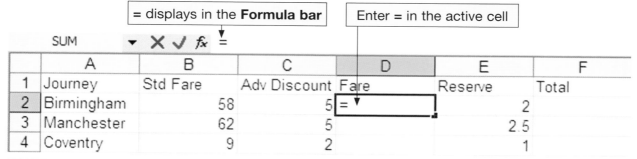

= displays in the **Formula bar**   Enter = in the active cell

	A	B	C	D	E	F
1	Journey	Std Fare	Adv Discount Fare		Reserve	Total
2	Birmingham	58	5	=	2	
3	Manchester	62	5		2.5	
4	Coventry	9	2		1	

FIGURE 2.36 The = sign is displayed in the **Formula bar** and in the active cell

4 Click in the cell that contains the first value (number).

5 The cell reference of that cell displays in the **Formula bar** and in the active cell (Figure 2.37).

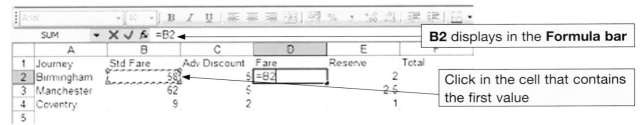

FIGURE 2.37 The cell reference is displayed in the Formula bar and in the cell

6 Use the keyboard to enter the correct mathematical operator (Figure 2.38).

	A	B	C	D	E	F
1	Journey	Std Fare	Adv Discount	Fare	Reserve	Total
2	Birmingham	58	5	=B2-	2	
3	Manchester	62	5		2.5	
4	Coventry	9	2		1	
5						

FIGURE 2.38 Entering the correct mathematical operator

7 Click in the cell that contains the second value.

8 The cell reference of the second cell displays after the mathematical operator in the **Formula bar** and in the cell (Figure 2.39).

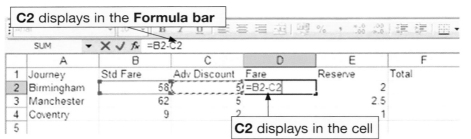

FIGURE 2.39 Selecting the second cell reference

9 Check the **Formula bar** to make sure that the formula is correct.

10 Press **Enter**, or click on the **Enter** tick ✔ on the **Formula bar**.

11 The calculation is made, and the result (the number) displays in the cell in which you created the formula.

12 Save the updated spreadsheet by clicking on the **Save** 🖫 icon.

1 Create a new spreadsheet.

2 Starting in cell **A1**, enter the data as shown below.

Journey	Std Fare	Adv Discount	Fare	Reserve	Total
Birmingham	58	5		2	
Manchester	62	5		2.5	
Coventry	9	2		1	

3 Widen the columns so that all data is displayed in full.

4 In cell **D2** create a formula to **subtract** the **Adv Discount** from the **Std Fare** for Birmingham.

5 Check the **Formula bar** – your formula should be =B2-C2.

6 In cell **F2** create a formula to **add** the **Fare** and the **Reserve** for Birmingham.

7 Check the **Formula bar** – your formula should be =D2+E2.

8 Insert your **name**, an **automatic date** and an **automatic filename** in the header or footer.

9 Save the spreadsheet using the filename **trains** in the folder **ssheets** you created earlier.

10 Keep the spreadsheet **trains** open.

Copying a formula

When you have created a formula for one set of data (e.g. in one row), you do not need to create the same formula again for the next set of data (e.g. for the next row) if it is to be calculated in the same way. You simply copy the formula into adjacent rows or columns.

When a formula is copied, the structure of the formula will remain the same, but Excel will automatically change the cell references. This is known as **relative cell referencing**.

In spreadsheets **copy** is referred to as **replicate**. You can replicate formulae across a row to the left or right (horizontally), or up and down a column (vertically).

▶▶ How to... *copy a formula*

Method 1: Using the fill handle

1 In your spreadsheet, click in the cell that contains the formula to be copied.

2 The bottom right-hand corner of the cell displays a black square.

3 Position the mouse pointer over the black square.

4 The mouse pointer changes to a **+** sign (Figure 2.40).

5 Drag the **+** sign over the cells where the formula is to be copied (Figure 2.41).

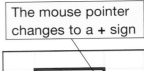

The mouse pointer changes to a + sign

FIGURE 2.40 Positioning the mouse pointer over the black square

	D2	▼	ƒx	=B2-C2		
	A	B	C	D	E	F
1	Journey	Std Fare	Adv Discount Fare		Reserve	Total
2	Birmingham	58	5	53	2	55
3	Manchester	62	5		2.5	
4	Coventry	9	2		1	
5						
6						

Drag the **+** sign over the cells

FIGURE 2.41 Copying the formula

6 The formula is copied to the selected cells.

Method 2: Copy and paste

1 In your spreadsheet, click in the cell that contains the formula you want to copy.

2 In the **Menu bar**, click on **Edit**.

3 From the **Edit** menu, click on **Copy**.

4 A flashing border called a **marquee** will appear around the cell that you have copied.

5 Highlight the cells where the formula is to be copied to.

6 Click again on the **Edit** menu.

7 Click on **Paste** in the menu.

8 The formula is copied to the highlighted cells.

9 Press the **Enter** key and the marquee will disappear.

TIP!

Double-click on the black square, and Excel will automatically fill the formula into the appropriate cells.

When using the fill handle, a **Smart Tag** (square icon) displays. Ignore this, it will disappear.

TIP!

Remember to save the updated spreadsheet by clicking on the **Save** icon.

Check your understanding Copy (replicate) formulae

1 In your spreadsheet **trains**, copy (replicate):

  a the formula in cell **D2** into cells **D3** and **D4**

  b the formula in cell **F2** into cells **F3** and **F4**.

2 Save your spreadsheet keeping the filename **trains**.

3 Your spreadsheet should look like the one in Figure 2.42.

4 Close the spreadsheet.

	A	B	C	D	E	F	G
1	Journey	Std Fare	Adv Discount Fare		Reserve	Total	
2	Birmingham	58	5	53	2	55	
3	Manchester	62	5	57	2.5	59.5	
4	Coventry	9	2	7	1	8	
5							

FIGURE 2.42 The spreadsheet **trains**

Creating functions

If the instruction is to use a function, you must use a function rather than a formula, even though it may be possible to perform the calculation using a formula.

▶▶ How to...   use the SUM function

There are several ways to create the **SUM** function in Excel. Read through all the instructions that follow, then complete 'Check your understanding: Create a spreadsheet and use the SUM function' on page 32 using each of the three methods. You will then be able to decide which method you prefer.

Method 1: Enter function in cell

1 In the spreadsheet, click in the cell where the calculation is to be carried out.

2 Enter the = sign.

3 Enter the word **SUM** followed by an opening bracket, i.e. **SUM(**

4 **=SUM(** displays in the **Formula bar** and in the active cell (Figure 2.43).

	A	B	C	D	E	F	G	H	I
					SUM ▾ ✕ ✓ ƒx =SUM(				
1	Language Courses								
2		Term 1	Term 2	Term 3	Yearly Fee	Discount	Admin	Amount Due	
3	French	20	18	15	=SUM(		0.95		
4	German	22	20	17	SUM(**number1**, [number2], ...)		0.75		
5	Spanish	24	21	18			0.5		
6	Arabic	28	26	21			0.6		
7	Average								
8									

FIGURE 2.43 =SUM(is displayed in the Formula bar and the cell

5 Highlight the range of cells to be added starting with the first cell and ending with the last cell.

6 **=SUM(B3:D3** displays in the **Formula bar** and in the cell (Figure 2.44). The cell references in other calculations will be the first and last cell that you highlighted with a colon between the cell references.

	A	B	C	D	E	F	G	H	I
					SUM ▾ ✕ ✓ ƒx =SUM(B3:D3				
1	Language Courses								
2		Term 1	Term 2	Term 3	Yearly Fee	Discount	Admin	Amount Due	
3	French	20	18	15	=SUM(B3:D3		0.95		
4	German	22	20	17	SUM(**number1**, [number2], ...)		0.75		
5	Spanish	24	21	18			0.5		
6	Arabic	28	26	21			0.6		
7	Average								
8									

FIGURE 2.44 =SUM(B3:D3 is displayed in the Formula bar and in the cell

7 Enter a closing bracket **)**

8 **=SUM(B3:D3)** displays in the **Formula bar** and in the cell (Figure 2.45). Remember that the cell references in other calculations will be different.

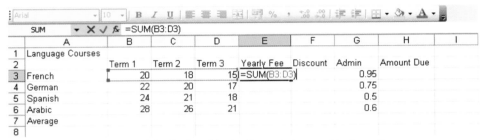

FIGURE 2.45 =SUM(B3:D3) is displayed in the Formula bar and in the cell

TIP!

The cell references will be different in other spreadsheets.

9 Check the **Formula bar** to make sure the formula is correct.

10 Press **Enter**, or click on the **Enter** tick ✓ on the **Formula bar**.

11 The calculation is made, and the result (the total) will display in the cell in which you created the function.

TIP!

If the formula is incorrect click **Cancel** ✗ on the **Formula bar** and start again.

Method 2: Insert function

1 In the spreadsheet, click in the cell where the calculation is to be carried out.

2 Click the *fx* **Insert Function** icon on the **Formula Bar** (Figure 2.46).

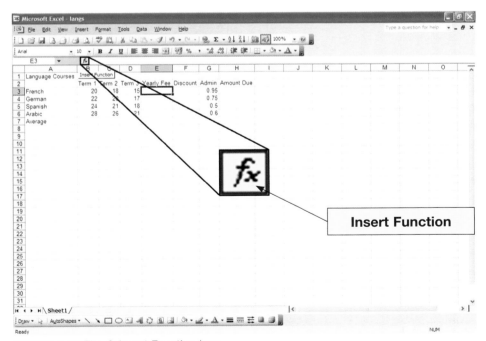

FIGURE 2.46 The *fx* Insert Function icon

3 An **Insert Function** dialogue box is displayed (Figure 2.47).

4 Click on **SUM**.

5 Click on **OK**.

6 A **Function Arguments** dialogue box appears (Figure 2.48).

7 In the **Number1** box the range of cells displays. Check this range is correct.

8 Click on **OK**.

9 The calculation is made, and the result (the total) will display in the cell in which you created the function.

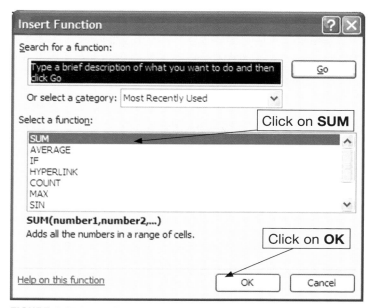

FIGURE 2.47 Insert Function dialogue box

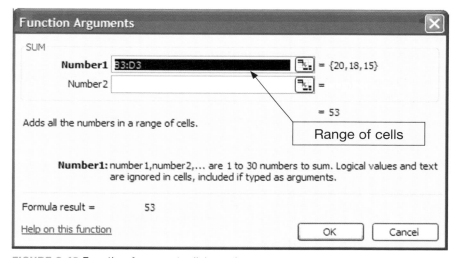

FIGURE 2.48 Function Arguments dialogue box

TIP!

If the range of cells shown is incorrect, highlight the correct range in the spreadsheet. Click and drag the blue title bar of the dialogue box to see the spreadsheet if required.

Method 3: AutoSum

Addition is the most frequently used function, so there is an **AutoSum** Σ icon on the **Standard toolbar** that creates the **SUM** function automatically. There is more than one way to use **AutoSum**, but the best way is outlined below.

1 Highlight the range of cells to be added AND the blank cell in which the result of the calculation is to be displayed.

2 Click on the **AutoSum** Σ icon.

3 The result of the calculation is displayed in what was the blank cell.

TIP!

Do not click the AutoSum icon to start every formula as this inserts **SUM** in front of every formula. The **SUM** function must only be used for adding a range of cells that are next to each other. **SUM** must not appear in any other formula.

1 Create a new spreadsheet.

2 Set the page orientation to **landscape**.

3 Starting in cell **A1**, enter the data as shown below.

Language Courses							
	Term 1	Term 2	Term 3	Yearly Fee	Discount	Admin	Amount Due
French	20	18	15			0.95	
German	22	20	17			0.75	
Spanish	24	21	18			0.5	
Arabic	28	26	21			0.6	
Average							

4 Widen all columns to display all data in full.

Using Method 1: Enter function in cell

5 In cell **E3**, use the **SUM** function to calculate the total **Yearly Fee** for the **French** row (the sum of cells **B3** to **D3**).

6 Check your function, it should be **=SUM(B3:D3)**

Using Method 2: Insert function

7 In cell **E4**, use the **SUM** function to calculate the total **Yearly Fee** for the **German** row (the sum of cells **B4** to **D4**).

8 Check your function, it should be **=SUM(B4:D4)**

Using Method 3: AutoSum

9 In cell **E5**, use the **SUM** function to calculate the total **Yearly Fee** for the **Spanish** row (the sum of cells **B5** to **D5**)

10 Check your function, it should be **=SUM(B5:D5)**

11 Copy the function from cell **E5** into cell **E6**.

12 Save your spreadsheet using the filename **langs** in the folder **ssheets**. Keep your spreadsheet open.

TIP!

From now on, when using the **SUM** function, use the method that you prefer.

1 In cell **F3**, create a formula to divide the **Yearly Fee** by **10**.

2 Check the **Formula bar**, your formula should be **=E3/10**

3 Copy the formula from cell **F3** into **F4**, **F5**, **F6**.

4 Insert your **name**, an **automatic date** and an **automatic filename** in the header or footer.

5 Save your spreadsheet, keeping the filename **langs**, in the folder **ssheets**.

6 Your spreadsheet should look like the one in Figure 2.49.

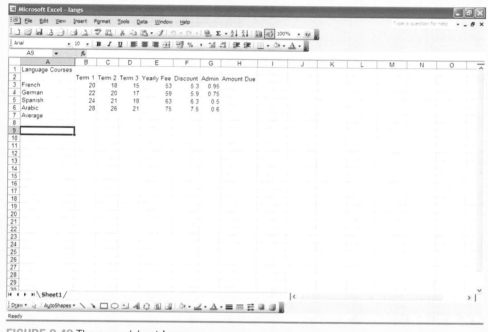

FIGURE 2.49 The spreadsheet langs

7 Keep the spreadsheet **langs** open.

▶▶ How to... *use the AVERAGE function*

There are several ways to create the **AVERAGE** function in Excel.

Method 1: Enter function in cell

1 In the spreadsheet, click in the cell in which the calculation is to be carried out.

2 Enter the = sign.

3 Enter the word **AVERAGE** followed by an opening bracket, i.e. **AVERAGE(**

TIP!

The word **AVERAGE** may be entered in upper or lower case.

4 =**AVERAGE(** displays in the **Formula bar** and in the cell (Figure 2.50).

5 Highlight the range of cells to be averaged starting with the first cell and ending with the last cell.

6 =**AVERAGE(B3:B6** displays in the **Formula bar** and in the cell (Figure 2.51). The cell references in other calculations will be the first and last cell that you highlighted with a colon between the cell references.

7 Enter a closing bracket **)**

8 =**AVERAGE(B3:B6)** displays in the **Formula bar** and in the cell (Figure 2.52). Remember that the cell references in other calculations will be different.

9 Check the **Formula bar** to make sure the formula is correct.

10 Press **Enter**, or click on the **Enter** tick ✔ on the **Formula bar**.

11 The calculation is made, and the result (the average figure) will display in the cell in which you created the function.

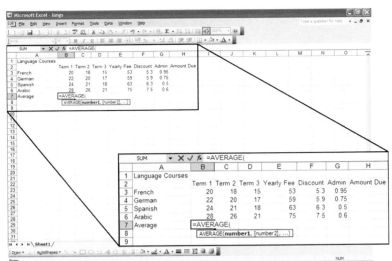

FIGURE 2.50 =AVERAGE(is displayed in the Formula Bar and in the cell

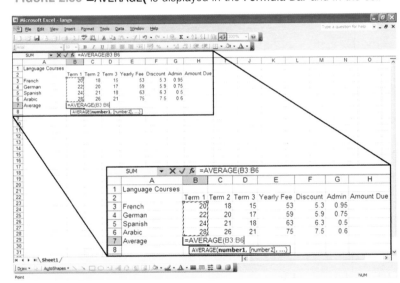

FIGURE 2.51 =AVERAGE(B3:B6 is displayed in the Formula bar and in the cell

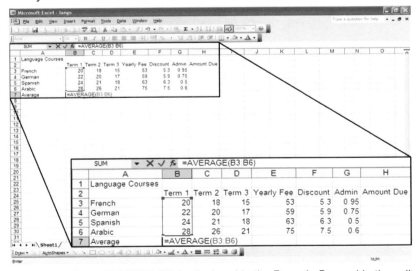

FIGURE 2.52 =AVERAGE(B3:B6) is displayed in the Formula Bar and in the cell

TIP!

The cell references will be different in other spreadsheets.

Method 2: Insert function

1 In the spreadsheet, click in the cell where the calculation is to be carried out.

2 Click on the **fx Insert Function** icon on the **Formula bar** (Figure 2.53).

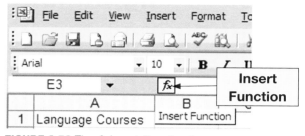

FIGURE 2.53 The *fx* Insert Function icon

3 An **Insert Function** dialogue box is displayed (Figure 2.54).

4 Click on the word **AVERAGE**.

5 Click on **OK**.

6 A **Function Arguments** dialogue box appears (Figure 2.55).

7 In the **Number1** box the range of cells displays. Check this range is correct.

8 Click on **OK**.

9 The calculation is made, and the result (the average) will display in the cell in which you created the function.

TIP!

If the range of cells shown is incorrect, highlight the correct range in the spreadsheet.

Method 3: AutoSum

1 Highlight the range of cells to be averaged AND the blank cell in which the result of the calculation is to be displayed.

2 Click on the **down arrow** next to the **AutoSum** Σ · icon on the **Standard toolbar**.

3 From the menu, click on **Average** (Figure 2.56).

4 The result of the calculation is displayed in what was the blank cell.

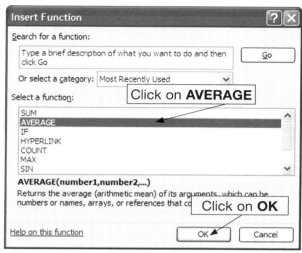

FIGURE 2.54 Insert Function dialogue box

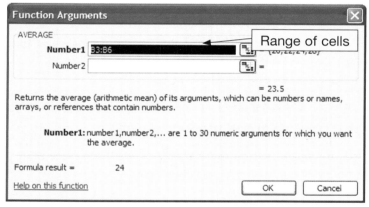

FIGURE 2.55 Function Arguments dialogue box

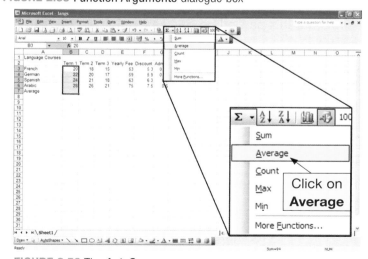

FIGURE 2.56 The AutoSum menu

1 In your spreadsheet **langs**, use each of the three methods below to create a formula using the **AVERAGE** function.

Using Method 1: Enter function in cell

2 Click in the **Average** row, in the **Term 1** column.

3 Use a function to calculate the **AVERAGE** of the **Term 1** figures for the four Language Courses.

Using Method 2: Insert function

4 Click in the **Average** row, in the **Term 2** column.

5 Use a function to calculate the **AVERAGE** of the **Term 2** figures for the four Language Courses.

Using Method 3: AutoSum (Average)

6 Click in the **Average** row, in the **Term 3** column.

7 Use a function to calculate the **AVERAGE** of the **Term 3** figures for the four Language Courses.

TIP!

From now on. when using the **AVERAGE** function, use the method you prefer.

8 Replicate (copy) the **AVERAGE** formula into the other cells starting from **Yearly Fee** up to **Admin**.

9 Save your spreadsheet keeping the filename **langs**.

Using brackets in a formula with more than one mathematical operator

You may need to use more than one mathematical operator * / + - in a formula. If so, you must use **brackets**.

If you need to use add or subtract and then multiply or divide, you *must* use brackets around the cells to be added or subtracted, so that Excel carries out this part of the calculation first, before carrying out the multiply or divide.

▶▶ How to... *use brackets in a formula*

1 In the spreadsheet, click in the cell where the formula is to be created.

2 Enter the = sign.

3 Enter an opening bracket (

4 Click in the cell that contains the first value (number).

5 The cell reference displays in the **Formula bar**.

6 Enter the correct mathematical operator.

7 Click in the cell that contains the second value.

8 The cell reference displays after the mathematical operator.

9 Enter a closing bracket **)**

10 Enter the correct mathematical operator after the bracket.

11 Click in the cell that contains the third value.

12 Check the **Formula bar** to make sure the formula is correct (Figure 2.57).

13 Press **Enter**, or click on the **Enter** tick 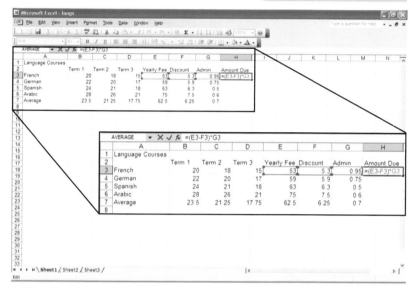 on the **Formula bar**.

14 The calculation is made, and the result (the value) will be displayed in the cell in which you created the formula.

FIGURE 2.57 Using brackets in a formula

Check your understanding *Create a formula using brackets*

1 In your spreadsheet **langs**, in cell **H3** create a formula as follows:

(Yearly Fee subtract Discount) multiply by Admin.

2 Check your formula, it should be: **=(E3-F3)*G3**. If you do not use brackets, you will get an incorrect result!

3 Replicate (copy) the formula from cell **H3** into cells **H4**, **H5**, **H6**.

4 Replicate (copy) the **AVERAGE** function from cell **G7** into cell **H7**.

5 Save your spreadsheet, keeping the filename **langs**. It should look similar to one in Figure 2.58.

6 Keep the spreadsheet open.

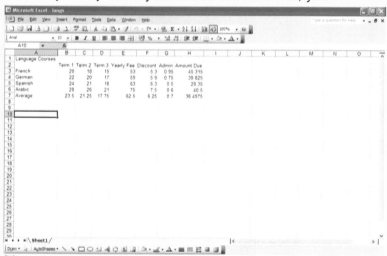

FIGURE 2.58 The spreadsheet **langs**

Spreadsheet print options

▶▶ How to... *set the spreadsheet print options*

1 In the **Menu bar**, click on **File**.

2 From the **File** menu, click on **Page Setup**.

3 The **Page Setup** dialogue box is displayed (Figure 2.59).

4 Check the **Page** tab is selected.

5 Check the orientation is set correctly.

6 In the **Scaling** section, click in the **Fit to** button.

7 In the **Fit to** boxes, check **1** is displayed in both **page(s) wide by ... tall** boxes.

8 Click on **OK** to set the print options.

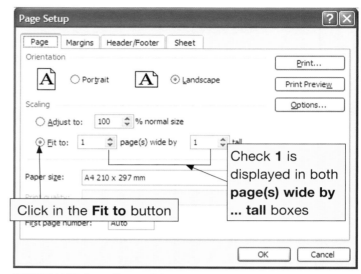

FIGURE 2.59 Page Setup dialogue box

Printing a spreadsheet

▶▶ How to... *print a spreadsheet*

1 In the **Menu bar**, click on **File**.

2 From the **File** menu, click on **Print** (Figure 2.60).

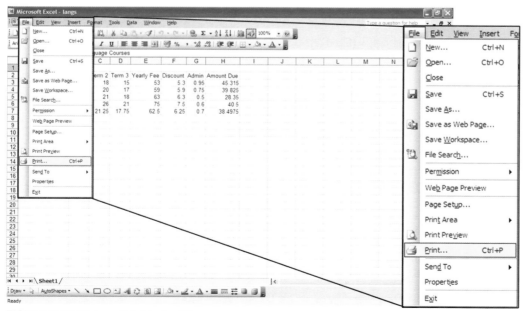

FIGURE 2.60 Click on Print in the File menu

3 The **Print** dialogue box is displayed (Figure 2.61).

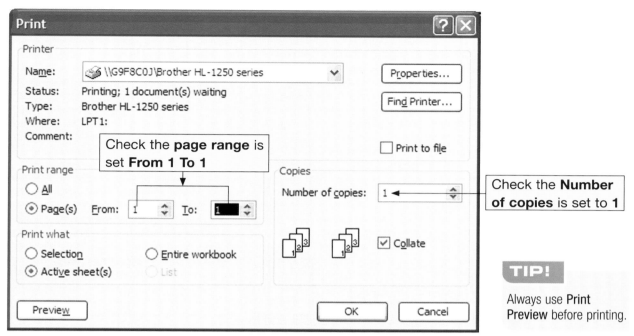

FIGURE 2.61 **Print** dialogue box

4 Check the **Page range** is set **From 1 To 1**.

5 Check the **Number of copies** is set to **1**.

6 Click on **OK** to print the spreadsheet.

FIGURE 2.62 **Print Preview** buttons

TIP!

Always use **Print Preview** before printing.

TIP!

Once you have checked the print settings, the next time you print a spreadsheet, click on the **Print Preview** icon on the **Standard toolbar**, then click on **Print** in the **Preview** window (Figure 2.62).

Check your understanding *Print spreadsheets*

1 In your spreadsheet **langs**, set the spreadsheet to fit to **1** page wide and **1** page tall.

2 Use **Print Preview** to check the spreadsheet and the headers and footers.

3 Save the spreadsheet keeping the filename **langs**.

4 Print the spreadsheet.

5 Close the spreadsheet. You will continue working on this spreadsheet in Section 2.

6 Check your printout against the solutions which can be found on the CD-ROM in the folder **ss_worked_copies**.

ASSESS YOUR SKILLS – Create a new spreadsheet

By working through Section 1 you will have learnt the skills listed below. Read each item to help you decide how confident you feel about each skill.

- start Excel
- open a blank spreadsheet
- enter data into a spreadsheet
- widen columns to make sure that all data is fully displayed
- set the orientation
- set the margins
- save a spreadsheet with a specified filename into a folder from within Excel
- insert headers and footers
- insert an automatic date in headers and footers
- insert an automatic filename in headers and footers
- check your work for accuracy
- save an updated spreadsheet
- close a spreadsheet
- understand the difference between formulae and functions
- create basic formulae using mathematical operators
- copy (replicate) formulae
- use the **SUM** function
- use the **AVERAGE** function
- create formulae using brackets
- use **Print Preview**
- set the print options (fit to one page, orientation, number of copies)
- print a spreadsheet with all data displayed in full.

If you think you need more practice on any of the skills above, go back and work through the skill(s) again.

If you feel confident, move on to Section 2.

LEARNING OUTCOMES

In this section you will learn how to:

- ○ open a saved spreadsheet
- ○ save an existing spreadsheet with a new filename
- ○ amend text and numeric data
- ○ understand automatic recalculation of data
- ○ insert a new column and enter data
- ○ insert a new row and enter data
- ○ delete a column
- ○ delete a row
- ○ align text and numbers
- ○ format numeric data
- ○ display gridlines
- ○ display borders and shading
- ○ display formulae in full
- ○ display row and column headings
- ○ print formulae
- ○ close a spreadsheet
- ○ exit from Excel.

Opening and saving an existing spreadsheet

▶▶ How to... *open a saved spreadsheet*

1 In the **Menu** bar, click on **File**.

2 From the **File** menu, click on **Open** (Figure 2.63).

3 The **Open** dialogue box is displayed (Figure 2.64).

4 In the **Look in** box, click on the **down arrow** to show a list of user areas. Click on your user area.

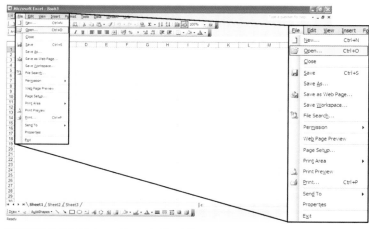

FIGURE 2.63 Click on **Open** in the **File** menu

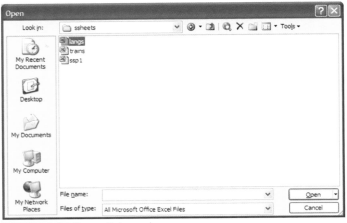

FIGURE 2.64 Open dialogue box

5 Click on the folder where the file is saved to open it.

6 Click on the required file.

7 Click on **Open**.

8 The selected file opens in Excel.

TIP!

Alternatively, click on the **Open** 📂 icon on the **Standard toolbar** to display the **Open** dialogue box.

Check your understanding *Open existing spreadsheets*

1 Open your saved spreadsheet **ssp1**.

2 Print the spreadsheet **ssp1**.

3 Close the file.

4 Open your saved spreadsheet **trains**.

5 Print the spreadsheet **trains**.

6 Close the file.

▶▶ How to... *save an existing spreadsheet with a new filename into an existing folder from within Excel*

1 In the **Menu** bar, click on **File**.

2 From the **File** menu, click on **Save As**.

3 The **Save As** dialogue box is displayed.

4 Click on the **down arrow** to the right of the **Save in** box, then click on your user area.

5 Double-click on the name of the folder you have already created.

TIP!

Always save your spreadsheets into folders to keep your files organised instead of saving all your files into one area.

6 The folder opens (Figure 2.65).

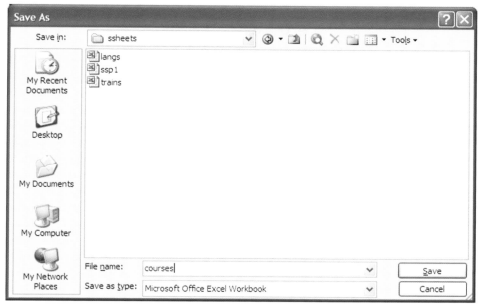

FIGURE 2.65 Save As dialogue box

7 In the **File name** box, enter the new filename.

8 Click on **Save** to save the file with a new filename.

Check your understanding
Open and save a spreadsheet into an existing folder

1 Open your saved spreadsheet **langs**.

2 Save it into your existing folder **ssheets** using the new filename **courses**.

Amending text and numeric data

You may be required to change (amend) the text or numbers in the cells in a spreadsheet.

▶▶ How to...   *amend (change) data (1)*

Replace all the existing data in a cell

1 In the spreadsheet, click once in the cell to be amended.

2 Enter the new data (text or numbers).

3 The existing data is replaced (you type over it).

4 Move to another cell.

5 When a number is changed any calculations using that number will automatically update. Check to make sure!

1 In your file **courses**, amend the column label **Discount** to **Rebate**.

2 Amend the **Term 1** figure for **Arabic** to **18**.

3 Check your previous printout of the spreadsheet **langs** to make sure that the **Average**, **Yearly Fee**, **Rebate** and **Amount Due** figures for Arabic have recalculated.

4 Save the spreadsheet keeping the filename **courses**.

▶▶ How to... *amend (change) data (2)*

Replace part of the data in a cell

1 In the spreadsheet, double-click in the cell to be amended.

2 A cursor displays in the cell.

3 Delete only the data to be replaced.

4 Enter the new data.

5 Move to another cell.

6 If you amend part of a number, check to make sure that any calculations using that number are automatically updated.

1 In your file **courses**, amend the cell **Language Courses** to **Languages**.

2 Amend the **Term 2** figure for **French** to **16**.

3 Save your spreadsheet keeping the filename **courses**.

Inserting data

After a spreadsheet has been created, it may be necessary to add data. In Excel, rows and columns can easily be added without the need to create the spreadsheet again.

▶▶ How to... *insert a new column*

1 In the spreadsheet, click anywhere in the column where the new column is to be inserted.

2 This column may contain data, don't worry, you will not delete this data – Excel will automatically move this column to the right when the new column is inserted.

TIP!

New columns are inserted to the left of the active cell.

3 In the **Menu bar**, click on **Insert**.

4 Click on **Columns** (Figure 2.66).

5 A new blank column is inserted and the subsequent columns are automatically relabelled.

6 Enter the required data in the new column.

7 Save the updated spreadsheet.

8 Check to see that any calculations have been updated. Excel does this automatically, but it is good practice to check.

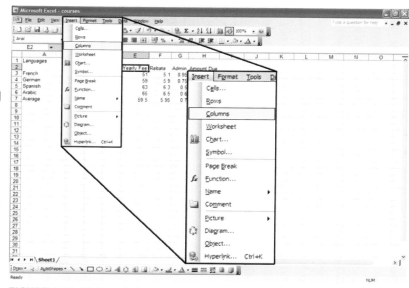

FIGURE 2.66 Click on **Columns** in the **Insert** menu

Below is an alternative, quick way to insert a column.

1 Right-click in the grey column letter where the new column is to be inserted.

2 The entire column is highlighted and a menu is displayed.

3 From the menu, click on **Insert** (Figure 2.67).

4 The new column is inserted.

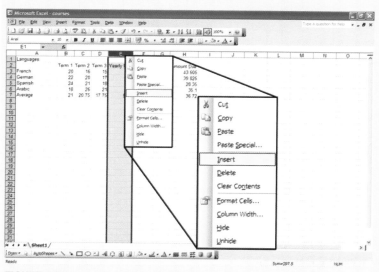

FIGURE 2.67 Inserting a new column

1 In your spreadsheet **courses**, insert a new column as column **E** between **Term 3** and **Yearly Fee**.

2 Enter the data in the new column **E** as shown below (Taster column).

Languages				
	Term 1	Term 2	Term 3	Taster
French	20	16	15	30
German	22	20	17	22
Spanish	24	21	18	25
Arabic	18	26	21	17
Average	21	20.75	17.75	

3 Save your spreadsheet keeping the filename **courses**.

▶▶ How to... *insert a new row*

1 In the spreadsheet, click anywhere in the row where the new row is to be inserted.

2 This row may contain data. Don't worry, you will not delete this data – Excel will automatically move this row below the inserted row.

3 In the **Menu bar**, click on **Insert** (Figure 2.68).

4 Click on **Rows**.

5 A new blank row is inserted and the subsequent rows are automatically renumbered.

6 Enter the required data in the new row.

7 Save the updated spreadsheet.

8 Check to see that any calculations have been updated. Although Excel does this automatically, it is good practice to check.

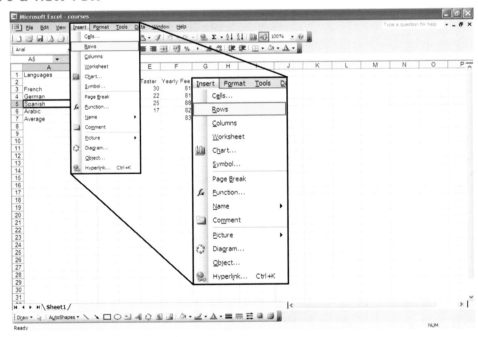

FIGURE 2.68 Click on **Rows** in the **Insert** menu

Below is an alternative, quick way to insert a row.

1 Right-click in the grey row number where the new row is to be inserted.

2 The entire row is highlighted and a menu is displayed.

3 From the menu, click on **Insert** (Figure 2.69).

4 The new row is inserted.

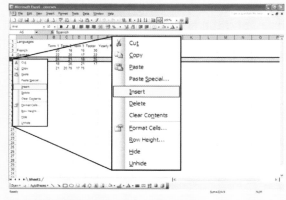

FIGURE 2.69 Inserting a new row

Check your understanding
Insert a new row and replicate formulae

1 In your spreadsheet **courses**, insert a new row between **German** and **Spanish** as new row **5**.

2 Enter the data in the new row as shown below (Italian row).

Languages								
	Term 1	Term 2	Term 3	Taster	Yearly Fee	Rebate	Admin	Amount Due
French	20	16	15	30	81	8.1	0.95	69.255
German	22	20	17	22	81	8.1	0.75	54.675
Italian	19	18	16	18			0.55	

3 Save your spreadsheet.

4 Replicate (copy) the formula in the **German** row for **Yearly Fee**, **Rebate** and **Amount Due** into the **Italian** row.

5 Copy the **Average** formula for **Term 3** into the **Taster** column.

6 Save your spreadsheet keeping the filename **courses**.

7 Your spreadsheet should look similar to the one in Figure 2.70. The figures in column **I** and row 8 may be formatted slightly differently.

	A	B	C	D	E	F	G	H	I	J
1	Languages									
2		Term 1	Term 2	Term 3	Taster	Yearly Fee	Rebate	Admin	Amount Due	
3	French	20	16	15	30	81	8.1	0.95	69.255	
4	German	22	20	17	22	81	8.1	0.75	54.675	
5	Italian	19	18	16	18	71	7.1	0.55	35.145	
6	Spanish	24	21	18	25	88	8.8	0.5	39.6	
7	Arabic	18	26	21	17	82	8.2	0.6	44.28	
8	Average	20.6	20.2	17.4	22.4	80.6	8.06	0.67	48.591	
9										

FIGURE 2.70 The spreadsheet **courses**

Deleting a row or a column of data

When deleting a row or a column, the entire row or column must be removed from the spreadsheet, and the subsequent row numbers or column letters will automatically readjust. Make sure that you do not delete only the contents of the cells in the row or column leaving behind a blank row or column.

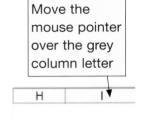

FIGURE 2.71 The column to be deleted

▶▶ How to... *delete a column*

1 In the spreadsheet, move the mouse pointer over the grey column letter of the column to be deleted (Figure 2.71).

2 Right-click with the mouse.

3 The entire column will be highlighted.

4 A drop-down menu is displayed (Figure 2.72).

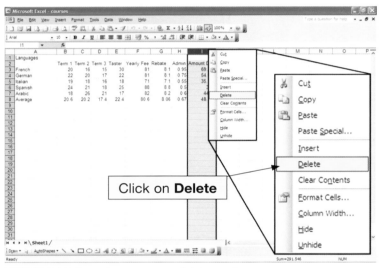

FIGURE 2.72 Drop-down menu to delete a column

5 Click on **Delete**.

6 The column is deleted and the letters of the remaining columns are automatically relabelled.

7 When a column is deleted, any calculation using numbers in the deleted column will automatically recalculate. Check to make sure!

8 Save the updated spreadsheet.

Check your understanding *Delete a column*

1 In your file **courses**, delete the **Amount Due** column and all its contents.

2 Save your spreadsheet using the new filename **newplan** in a new folder called **sect2**.

1 In your spreadsheet, move the mouse pointer over the grey row number to be deleted (Figure 2.73).

2 Right-click with the mouse.

3 The entire row will be highlighted.

4 A drop-down menu is displayed (Figure 2.74).

5 Click on **Delete**.

6 The row is deleted and the numbers of the remaining rows are automatically renumbered.

7 When a row is deleted, any calculation using numbers in the deleted row will automatically recalculate. Check to make sure!

8 Save the updated spreadsheet.

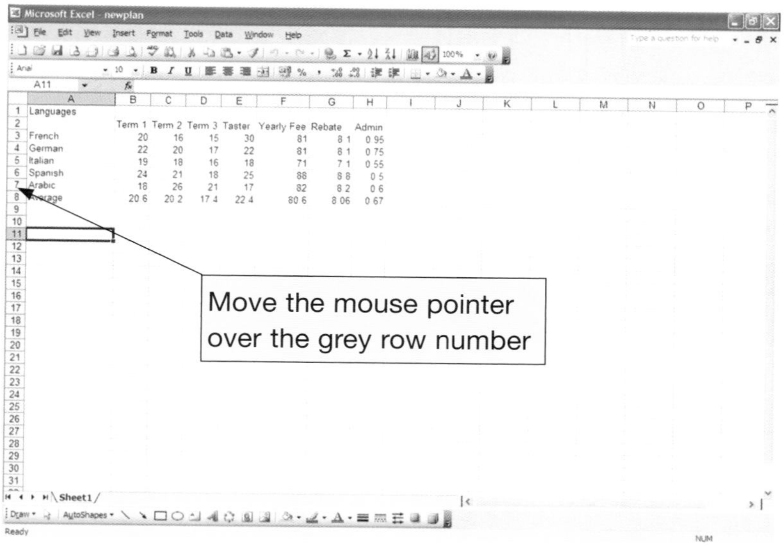

FIGURE 2.73 The row to be deleted

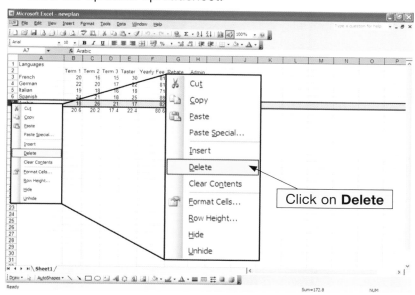

FIGURE 2.74 Drop-down menu to delete a row

Check your understanding *Delete a row*

1 In your file **newplan**, delete the row for **Arabic** and all its contents.

2 Make sure blank cells do not remain in between rows.

3 Save your spreadsheet keeping the filename **newplan**.

Alignment

FIGURE 2.75 Alignment icons on the **Formatting toolbar**

Alignment is how the data lines up with the left or right edge of the cell. Data in a cell can be aligned to the left, to the right or centre. Text is usually displayed left-aligned or centred, and numbers are usually displayed right-aligned. In Excel, when text is entered into a cell, it automatically aligns to the left, while numbers are automatically right-aligned (Figure 2.75).

LEFT-ALIGNED TEXT	CENTRED TEXT AND NUMBERS	RIGHT-ALIGNED TEXT AND NUMBERS
Course fees	Term 3	Total course fee
Word processing	15.00	53.00
Spreadsheets	18.00	60.00

Examples of alignment

▶▶ How to... *left-align data*

1 In the spreadsheet, highlight the cells to be left-aligned.

2 Click on the **Align Left** icon on the **Formatting toolbar.**

▶▶ How to... *right-align data*

1 In the spreadsheet, highlight the cells to be right-aligned.

2 Click on the **Align Right** icon on the **Formatting toolbar.**

▶▶ How to... *centre data*

1 In the spreadsheet, highlight the cells to be centred.

2 Click on the **Center** icon on the **Formatting toolbar.**

TIP!

To align one cell only, click in the cell then click the required alignment icon.

TIP!

It may be difficult to see on the screen how the text is aligned. To check line alignment, click in the relevant cell(s) and look at the **Left**, **Right** or **Center** alignment icons. The icon that appears to be 'switched on' (brighter shade) shows which alignment has been set.

Check your understanding   *Set the alignment*

1 In your file **newplan**, apply the following alignments:

   a Right-align all the column labels from **Term 1** to **Admin** (inclusive).

   b Right-align all the numbers in the spreadsheet.

2 Save the spreadsheet, keeping the filename **newplan**.

TIP!

Although numbers automatically display as right-aligned by default in Excel, it is best to highlight them and click the right-align icon.

Formatting numeric data

Numbers can be formatted so that their display changes but the actual value (number) remains the same. Common numeric formats are shown in the table opposite.

TYPE OF FORMAT	HOW FORMAT IS DISPLAYED	EXAMPLE
Integer	Whole number, no decimal places.	25
Two decimal places	A decimal point followed by two numbers without currency symbol.	25.00
Currency format	A currency symbol (e.g. the £ or € sign) precedes the numbers. The numbers can be displayed without decimal places or with two decimal places.	£25 or £25.00

Common numeric formats

▶▶ How to... *format numbers to integer (no decimal places)*

1 In the spreadsheet, highlight the cells to be formatted.

2 Right-click anywhere within the highlighted cells.

3 A drop-down menu is displayed.

4 Click on **Format Cells** (Figure 2.76).

5 The **Format Cells** dialogue box is displayed (Figure 2.77).

TIP!

To format one cell only, click in the cell then right-click and select **Format Cells**.

TIP!

Below is an alternative, way to open the Format Cells dialogue box:

1 Highlight the relevant numbers.

2 In the **Menu** bar, click on **Format**.

3 From the **Format** menu, click on **Cells**.

4 The **Format Cells** dialogue box is displayed.

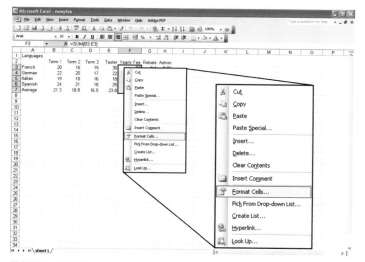

FIGURE 2.76 Drop-down menu to format cells

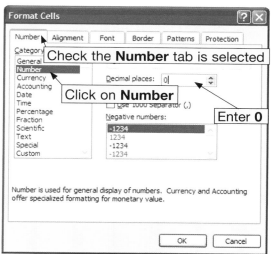

FIGURE 2.77 Format Cells dialogue box

6 Check the **Number** tab is selected.

7 In the **Category** list, click on **Number**.

8 In the **Decimal places** box, enter **0** (or use the **down arrow**).

9 Click on **OK** to format the numbers as whole numbers (integer).

What does it mean?

Decimal places
Decimal places refer to the numbers displayed after the decimal point.
○ The number 25.5 has 1 decimal place.
○ The number 25.54 has 2 decimal places.

▶▶ How to... *format numbers to a fixed number of decimal places*

1 In the spreadsheet, highlight the cells to be formatted.

2 Right-click anywhere within the highlighted cells.

3 A drop-down menu is displayed.

4 Click on **Format Cells**.

5 The **Format Cells** dialogue box is displayed (Figure 2.78).

6 Check the **Number** tab is selected.

7 In the **Category** list, click on **Number**.

8 In the **Decimal places** box, enter the required number of decimal places (or use the **up/down arrows**) (Figure 2.78).

9 Click on **OK**.

10 The numbers are displayed with decimal places.

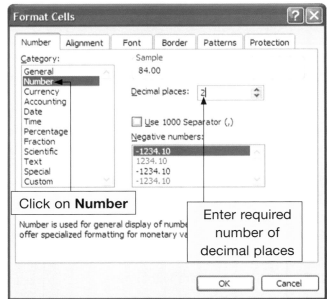

FIGURE 2.78 Format Cells dialogue box

TIP!

Use the Increase Decimal or Decrease Decimal icons on the formating toolbar.

▶▶ How to... *format numbers to currency*

1 In the spreadsheet, highlight the cells to be formatted.

2 Right-click anywhere within the highlighted cells.

3 A menu is displayed.

4 Click on **Format Cells**.

5 The Format Cells dialogue box is displayed (Figure 2.79).

FIGURE 2.79 Format Cells dialogue box

TIP!

Do not use the **Currency** icon on the **Formatting toolbar** as this will display the cell in accounting format.

What does it mean?

Currency
Currency is the type of money that is used in a country. When currency format is applied, any currency symbol may be displayed. In the UK, the currency symbol is £. € (Euro symbol) is also used in the UK.

6 Check the **Number** tab is selected.

7 In the **Category** list, click on **Currency**.

8 In the **Decimal places** box, enter the required number of decimal places (or use the **up/down arrows**).

9 In the **Symbol** box, click on the **down arrow** and click on the required currency format, e.g. £.

10 Click on **OK**.

11 The numbers are formatted with the currency symbol.

TIP!

If hash signs ##### display in cell(s), widen the column to display the data in full.

Check your understanding *Format numeric data*

1 In your file **newplan**, format the numeric data as follows.

   a Format all the figures in the **Yearly Fee** column with the **£** currency symbol to **0** decimal places.

   b Format all the figures in the **Rebate** and **Admin** columns with the **£** currency symbol to **2** decimal places.

TIP!

The currency symbol displayed should be appropriate to the country that you live in.

   c Format the figures in the **Average** row for **Term 1**, **Term 2**, **Term 3** and **Taster** to **2** decimal places with **no** currency symbol.

2 Save your spreadsheet keeping the filename **newplan**.

3 Your spreadsheet should look similar to the one in Figure 2.80.

	A	B	C	D	E	F	G	H	I
1	Languages								
2		Term 1	Term 2	Term 3	Taster	Yearly Fee	Rebate	Admin	
3	French	20	16	15	30	£81	£8.10	£0.95	
4	German	22	20	17	22	£81	£8.10	£0.75	
5	Italian	19	18	16	18	£71	£7.10	£0.55	
6	Spanish	24	21	18	25	£88	£8.80	£0.50	
7	Average	21.25	18.75	16.50	23.75	£80	£8.03	£0.69	
8									

FIGURE 2.80 The spreadsheet newplan

Borders, shading and gridlines

Borders give prominence to selected data in a spreadsheet. Borders are not the same as gridlines – gridlines display for all the data in the spreadsheet. However, borders can be set for selected cells to make these cells stand out. Borders can be used even if gridlines are displayed.

▶▶ How to... *add a border*

1 In the spreadsheet, highlight the cells to be framed with a border. To select one cell only click in the cell.

2 On the **Formatting toolbar**, click on the **down arrow** to the right of the **Borders** ▾ icon.

3 A drop-down selection displays the various border options (Figure 2.81).

4 Select the **Outside Border** or **Thick Box Border** option.

5 Click on the **Print Preview** 🔍 icon to check the border is displayed correctly.

TIP!

Select the Thick Box Border as this displays more clearly on a printout.

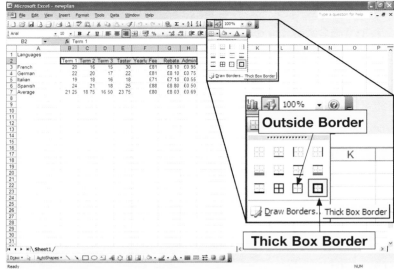

FIGURE 2.81 Border options menu

▶▶ How to... *shade cells*

1 In the spreadsheet, highlight the cells to be shaded. To shade one cell only click in the cell.

2 On the **Formatting toolbar**, click on the **down arrow** to the right of the **Fill Color** 🎨 ▼ icon.

3 A drop-down selection displays various fill colour options (Figure 2.82).

4 Click on a pale colour square.

5 The highlighted cells are filled with the selected colour.

6 Check the data in the shaded cells is still clearly readable.

7 Make sure that the shading is clearly visible on the printout.

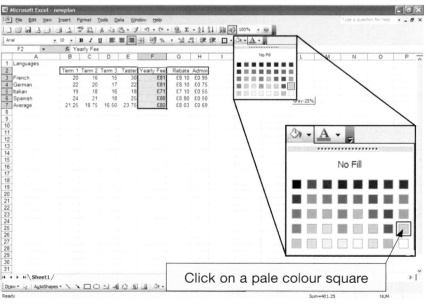

FIGURE 2.82 Fill Color menu

1 In your file **newplan**, add a single, thick outside border around all the column labels starting with **Term 1** and ending with **Admin** (inclusive).

2 Shade the column label and the numbers in the **Yearly Fee** column.

3 Save your spreadsheet keeping the filename **newplan**.

▶▶ How to... *display gridlines*

1 In the spreadsheet, click on the **File** menu.

2 From the menu, click on **Page Setup**.

3 The **Page Setup** dialogue box is displayed (Figure 2.83).

4 Click on the **Sheet** tab.

5 In the **Print** section, click in the **Gridlines** box to insert a tick.

6 Click on **OK**.

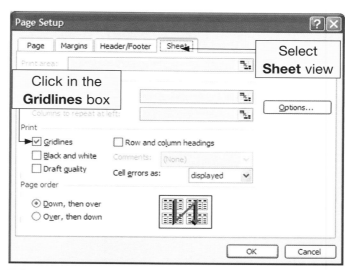

FIGURE 2.83 **Page Setup** dialogue box in **Sheet** view

TIP!

Click on the **Print Preview** icon to check gridlines are displayed.

1 In your file **newplan**, display gridlines.

2 Save the spreadsheet.

3 Print the spreadsheet.

4 Check your printout against the solution which can be found on the CD-ROM in the folder **ss_worked_copies**.

Displaying formulae

When formulae are used the actual values (numbers) display in the cell(s), and the formulae are in the background. If a cell containing a formula is clicked, the formula for that cell will display in the **Formula bar**. Printing the formulae proves that you have used formulae and functions correctly and that you have copied (replicated) the formulae and functions where instructed.

1 In the spreadsheet, click on the **Tools** menu (Figure 2.84).

2 From the menu, click on **Options**.

3 The **Options** dialogue box is displayed (Figure 2.85).

4 Check the **View** tab is selected.

5 In the **Window options** section, click in the **Formulas** box to insert a tick.

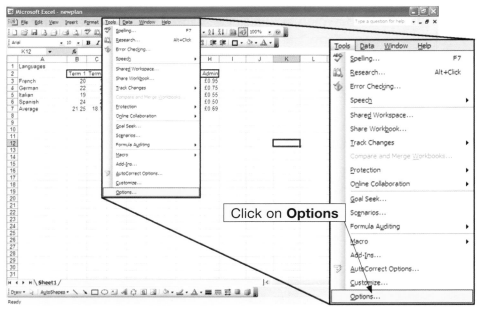

FIGURE 2.84 The Tools menu

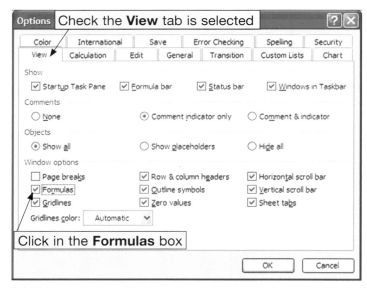

FIGURE 2.85 Options dialogue box

6 Click on **OK**.

7 The formulae are displayed on screen instead of the numbers. When formulae are displayed, columns become wider. However, you can adjust the width of all columns using **AutoFit**.

How to... *use AutoFit to adjust column widths*

1 Highlight the entire spreadsheet by clicking on the shaded cell to the left of the column letter **A** and above the row number **1** (Figure 2.86).

2 In the grey area displaying the column letters, position the mouse pointer over the vertical line dividing any two columns.

3 The mouse pointer changes into ↔.

4 Double-click with the left mouse button.

5 Excel automatically adjusts all the column widths to display all data in full.

When formulae are displayed, some formatting is lost, e.g. left and right alignment, decimal places, currency format, date format. This is normal. When you return to the spreadsheet view, all the formatting you had set will display again.

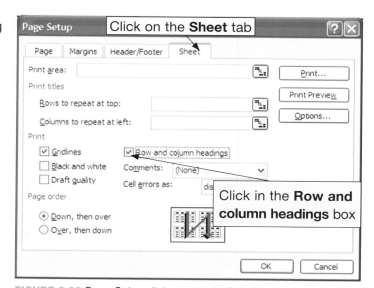

FIGURE 2.86 Highlight the spreadshet

Languages		Term 1	Term 2	Term 3	Taster	Yearly Fee	Rebate	Admin
French	20	16	15	30	=SUM(B3 E3)	=F3 10	0 95	
German	22	20	17	22	=SUM(B4 E4)	=F4 10	0 75	
Italian	19	18	16	18	=SUM(B5 E5)	=F5 10	0 55	
Spanish	24	21	18	25	=SUM(B6 E6)	=F6 10	0 5	
Average	=AVERAGE(B3 B6)	=AVERAGE(C3 C6)	=AVERAGE(D3 D6)	=AVERAGE(E3 E6)	=AVERAGE(F3:F6)	=AVERAGE(G3 G6)	=AVERAGE(H3 H6)	

FIGURE 2.87 All formulae are fully displayed

Row and column headings

Row and column headings are the column letters **A**, **B**, **C**, etc. and the row numbers **1**, **2**, **3**, etc. Do not confuse row and column headings with the row and column labels (titles) that you enter in the cells of the spreadsheet. Displaying row and column headings is normally required on a formula printout.

 **How to...** *display row and column headings on the printout*

1 In the spreadsheet, click on the **File** menu.

2 From the menu, click on **Page Setup**.

3 The **Page Setup** dialogue box is displayed (Figure 2.88).

4 Click on the **Sheet** tab.

FIGURE 2.88 **Page Setup** dialogue box in Sheet view

5 In the Print section, click in the **Row and column headings** box to insert a tick.

6 Click on **OK**.

TIP!

Click on the **Print Preview** icon to check row and column headings are displayed.

Formula print options

▶▶ How to... *set/check the formula print options*

1 In the spreadsheet, click on the **File** menu.

2 From the menu, click on **Page Setup**.

3 The **Page Setup** dialogue box is displayed (Figure 2.89).

4 Check the **Page** tab is selected.

5 Check the orientation is set correctly.

6 In the **Scaling** section, click in the **Fit to** button.

7 In the **Fit to** boxes, check **1** is displayed in both **page(s) wide by ... tall** boxes.

8 Click on **OK** to set the print options.

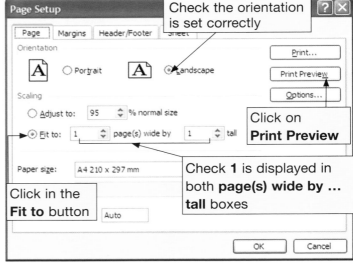

FIGURE 2.89 Page Setup dialogue box in Page view

Callouts in figure:
Check the orientation is set correctly
Click on **Print Preview**
Check **1** is displayed in both **page(s) wide by ... tall** boxes
Click in the **Fit to** button

Printing formulae

▶▶ How to... *print formulae*

1 In the spreadsheet, click on the **File** menu.

2 From the menu, click on **Print**.

3 The **Print** dialogue box is displayed.

4 Check the **Page Range** is set **From 1 To 1**.

5 Check the **Number of copies** is set to **1**.

6 Click on **OK** to print out the formulae.

TIP!

Always use **Print Preview** before printing.

TIP!

Alternatively, click on the **Print** icon on the **Standard** toolbar.

Check your understanding
Display formulae, row and column headings and print formulae

1 In your file **newplan**, display the formulae.

2 Adjust the column widths to make sure all formulae are fully displayed.

3 Set the formulae to print on **one page** in **landscape** orientation.

4 Display **row and column headings**.

5 Use **Print Preview** to check that you have carried out the instructions above.

6 Print the formulae on one page.

7 Save the formulae print using the new filename **npform** into the folder you created earlier called **sect2**.

8 Check your formulae printout against the solution which can be found on the CD-ROM in the folder **ss_worked_copies**.

Formula and spreadsheet views

▶▶ How to... *change from formula view to spreadsheet view*

1 In the spreadsheet, click on the **Tools** menu.

2 From the menu, click on **Options**.

3 An **Options** dialogue box is displayed.

4 Check the **View** tab is selected.

5 Click in the **Formulas** box to remove the tick.

6 Click on **OK** to return to spreadsheet view.

▶▶ How to... *display all spreadsheet data in full*

1 When the spreadsheet is displayed again after displaying formula, the columns may not be wide enough to display the data in full.

2 Highlight the entire spreadsheet by clicking on the shaded cell to the left of the column letter **A** and above the row number **1** (Figure 2.90).

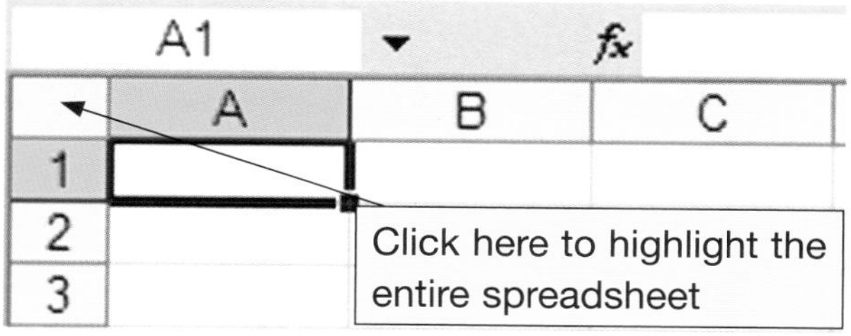

TIP!

To switch from spreadsheet view to formulae view and vice versa, press **Ctrl + `** key (**Accent** key usually above the **Tab** key).

TIP!

Another method is: Highlight the entire spreadsheet, click the **Format** menu, click on **Columns** and click on **AutoFit selection**.

FIGURE 2.90 Highlighting the entire spreadsheet

3 Position the mouse pointer over the vertical line dividing any two columns in the grey area displaying the column letters.

4 The mouse pointer changes into ↔.

5 Double-click with the left mouse button.

6 Excel automatically adjusts all the column widths to display the data in full.

Closing a spreadsheet

When you have saved and printed your document, you should close it. It is good practice to remember to close a file before you close a program.

▶▶ How to... *close a spreadsheet*

1 In the spreadsheet, click on the **File** menu.

2 From the menu, click on **Close**.

Exiting from Excel

When the spreadsheet has been closed you should exit from Excel.

▶▶ How to... *exit from Excel*

1 In the spreadsheet, click on the **File** menu.

2 From the menu, click on **Exit**.

TIP!

Alternatively, at the top right corner of the Excel window, click on the black cross to close the spreadsheet and the red cross to close Excel (Figure 2.91).

FIGURE 2.91 Closing the spreadsheet and exiting Excel

Check your understanding
Change from formula view to spreadsheet view and exit Excel

1 In your file **npform**.

2 Change the view from formulae back to the spreadsheet view.

3 Adjust the column widths using AutoFit to diplay all data in full.

4 Close the spreadsheet, do not save it again (you have previously saved **newplan** and **npform**).

5 Exit Excel.

ASSESS YOUR SKILLS – Edit a spreadsheet

By working through Section 2 you will have learnt the skills below. Read each item to help you decide how confident you feel about each skill.

- ○ open an existing spreadsheet
- ○ save an existing spreadsheet with a new filename into an existing folder from within Excel
- ○ amend text and numeric data
- ○ check that formulae automatically recalculate when data is amended
- ○ insert a new column and enter data
- ○ insert a new row and enter data
- ○ delete a column
- ○ delete a row
- ○ align text and numbers
- ○ format numeric data as integer (no decimal places) with a currency symbol, as integer with no currency symbol
- ○ display gridlines
- ○ display borders
- ○ shade cells
- ○ display formulae
- ○ check that all formulae are displayed in full
- ○ display row and column headings
- ○ print formulae with all formulae displayed in full
- ○ change the view to display the spreadsheet data
- ○ use **AutoFit** to display all spreadsheet data in full
- ○ close a spreadsheet
- ○ exit from Excel.

If you think you need more practice on any of the skills above, go back and work through the skill(s) again.

If you feel confident, move on to Chapter 2.

UNIT 2: Creating spreadsheets and graphs

Chapter 2   *Creating graphs*

In this chapter, you will learn how to create three types of graphs:

- ○ *pie charts*
- ○ *bar charts*
- ○ *line graphs.*

You will use Microsoft Office Excel 2003, which you have become familiar with in Chapter 1. We will refer to the program as Excel from now on. Default settings are assumed.

This chapter is divided into three sections:

- ○ *in Section 1, you will learn how to create pie charts*
- ○ *in Section 2, you will learn how to create bar charts including comparative bar charts*
- ○ *in Section 3, you will learn how to create line graphs including comparative line graphs.*

How to work through this chapter

1   Before you begin this unit, make sure you feel confident with the basics of using a computer and Windows XP. These skills are covered in Chapter 1 of the Unit 1 book *Learning to Pass New CLAiT: File management and e-document production*.

2   Read the explanation of a term first.

3   If there are some terms you do not understand, refer to the **Definition of terms** on the CD-ROM.

4   Work through the chapter in sequence so that one skill is understood before moving on to the next. This ensures thorough understanding of the topic and prevents unnecessary mistakes.

5   Read the ▶ *How to...* guidelines which give step-by-step instructions for each skill; do not attempt to work through them. Read through the points and look at the screenshots – make sure that you understand all the instructions before moving on.

6   To make sure that you have understood how to perform a skill, work through the **Check your understanding** task that follows. You should refer to the How to... instructions when doing the task.

7 At the end of each section is an **Assess your skills** table. This lists the skills that you will have practised by working through each section. Look at each item listed to help you decide whether you are confident that you can perform each skill.

8 At the end of the book there are **Quick reference guides**, **Build-up** and **Practice tasks**. Work through each task.

If you need help you may refer to the How to... guidelines or Quick reference guides whilst doing the Build-up tasks. Whilst working on the Practice tasks you should feel confident enough to use only the Quick reference guides if you need support. These guides may also be used during an assessment.

A CD-ROM accompanies this book. On it are the files required to create the graphs, which can be found in the folder **files_graphs**. The solutions for the creating graphs tasks can be found in the folder **graphs_worked_copies**.

Files for this chapter

To work through the tasks in this chapter, you will need the files from the folder **files_graphs**, which you will find on the CD-ROM provided with this book. Copy this folder into your user area before you begin.

▶▶ How to... *copy the folder files_graphs from the CD-ROM*

1 Make sure the computer is switched on and the desktop screen is displayed. Insert the CD-ROM into the CD-ROM drive of your computer.

2 Close any windows that may open.

3 On the desktop, double-click on the **My Computer** icon to display the **My Computer** window. The **My Computer** window is displayed.

4 Under **Devices with Removable Storage**, double-click on the **CD-ROM Drive** icon to view the contents of the CD-ROM.

5 Double-click on the **L1_Unit2_SS+GR** folder. Double-click on the **Source files** folder.

6 The **Source files** window displays (Figure 2.92).

7 Click on the folder **files_graphs**.

8 The folder will be highlighted (usually blue).

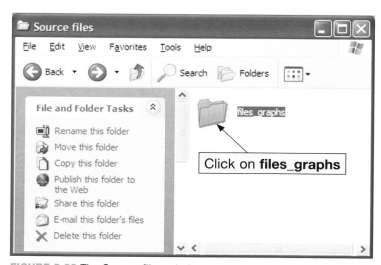

FIGURE 2.92 The Source files window

9   In the **File and Folder Tasks box**, click on **Copy this folder**.

10 The **Copy Items** dialogue box is displayed (Figure 2.93).

11 Click on the user area that you want to copy the folder **files_graphs** to.

12 Click on **Copy**.

13 The folder **files_graphs** is copied to your user area.

14 It is advisable to copy and paste a second copy of the file to another folder in your user area as backup.

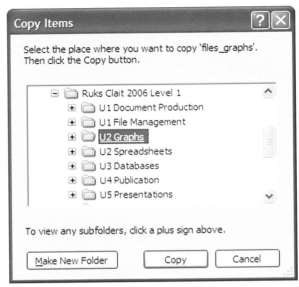

FIGURE 2.93 **Copy Items** dialogue box

1: Create a pie chart

LEARNING OUTCOMES

In this section you will learn how to:

- understand the types and purpose of graphs
- open a datafile from within Excel
- open a datafile from **My Computer**
- save a datafile with a new name
- view a datafile and identify data for a chart
- identify the parts of a pie chart
- select the data for a pie chart
- use the Chart Wizard to create a pie chart
- save an updated file
- print a chart
- understand legends
- understand the importance of distinctive data
- make sure that chart data is clearly distinctive (set the print options and fill sectors with patterns).

What are graphs?

Graphs are an effective way of presenting numeric data in a visual (graphical) form. By creating a graph, you can see particular trends or patterns, sale of products, differences in performances, etc. Sometimes it can be difficult to identify important information from a spreadsheet. A visual picture of the numbers often makes it easier to identify trends or changes in data.

Excel offers a wide range of graph styles and options to present data for different types of information. There are three common chart types.

- **Pie charts**. *Data is displayed as slices of a round pie. Each slice represents a proportion of the total.*
- **Bar charts**. *Data is displayed as vertical bars. The bars show comparisons between categories.*
- **Line graphs**. *Data is displayed as individual points joined by a line. The line shows trends over time or for categories.*

Charts make **comparison of data** much simpler and clearer and can make the data easier to understand.

Another advantage of graphs in Excel is that a graph is not a static (unchanging) picture. When the data in a spreadsheet is changed, the graph automatically updates. This is referred to as **live data modelling**.

Using the Chart Wizard makes creating graphs very simple as it guides you step-by-step, with a preview of the chart at each step. Once the graph has been created, changes can also be made to any part of the graph.

Now, using the skills that you learned in Unit 1 Chapter 1, switch on your computer and log in. Start Excel (to remind you how to do this, turn to pages 5–6 of this book).

Opening datafiles

A datafile can be opened from within Excel or from the **My Computer** window. Both methods are described below.

TIP!

Graphs are also referred to as charts.

What does it mean?

Datafile
A file that contains data. You will be supplied with a datafile which will contain the data needed to create the graph.

1   In Excel, click on **File** in the **Menu bar.**

2   From the **File** menu, click on **Open** (Figure 2.94).

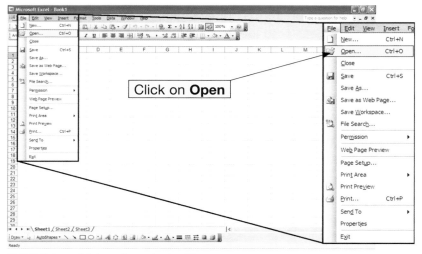

Click on **Open**

FIGURE 2.94 Click on Open in the File menu

3   The **Open** dialogue box displays (Figure 2.95).

4   Click on the **down arrow** next to the **Look in** box.

5   A list of user areas is displayed.

6   Find your user area and double-click on it.

7   Double-click on the folder in your user area where the file is saved.

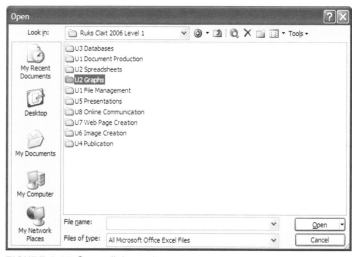

FIGURE 2.95 Open dialogue box

8   The folder opens and a list of files is displayed (Figure 2.96).

9   Click on the required file.

10 Click on **Open**.

11 The selected file opens in Excel.

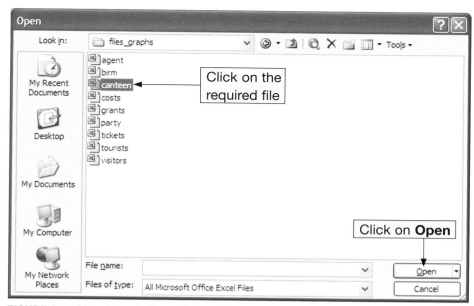

FIGURE 2.96 List of files in **Open** dialogue box

> **How to...** *open the datafile from My Computer*

1 On the desktop, double-click on the **My Computer** icon.

2 The **My Computer** window is displayed.

3 Go to your user area and double-click on it.

4 Double-click on the folder icon containing the files, e.g. **files_graphs**.

5 The list of files is displayed (Figure 2.97).

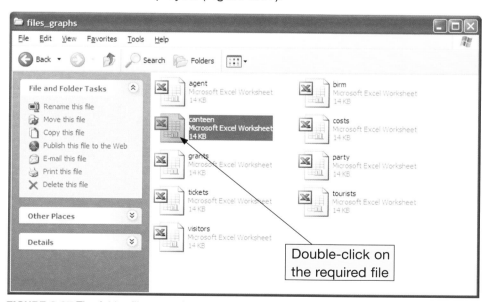

FIGURE 2.97 The folder files_graphs

6 Double-click on the required Excel file.

7 The file opens in Excel.

Saving datafiles

▶▶ How to... *save a datafile with a new filename into a new folder from within Excel*

1 In the **Menu bar**, click on **File**.

2 From the **File** menu, click on **Save As** (Figure 2.98).

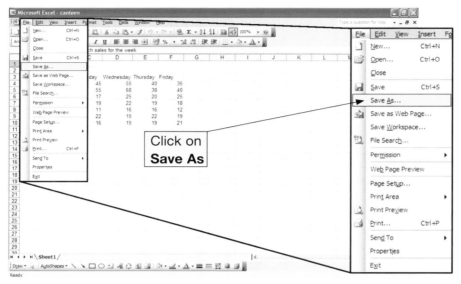

FIGURE 2.98 Click on **Save As** in the **File** menu

3 The **Save As** dialogue box is displayed (Figure 2.99).

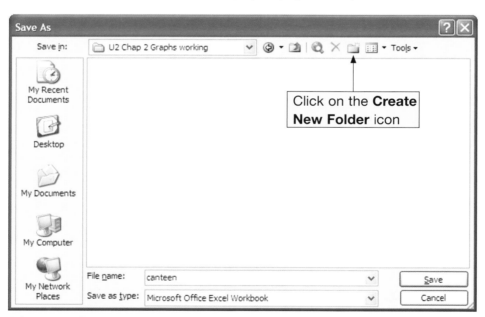

FIGURE 2.99 Save As dialogue box

4 Click on the **down arrow** to the right of the **Save in** box, then click on your user area.

5   Double-click to open the required subfolder(s).

6   The folder name displays in the **Save in** box.

7   Click on the **Create New Folder** icon.

8   A **New Folder** dialogue box is displayed (Figure 2.100).

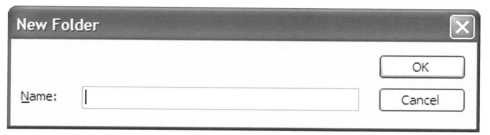

FIGURE 2.100 New Folder dialogue box

9   Enter the new folder name in the **Name** box.

10 Click on **OK** to create a new folder.

11 In the **Save As** dialogue box, in the **File name** box, delete the existing filename.

12 Enter the new filename.

13 Click on **Save**.

14 The file is saved with a new filename in a new folder within Excel.

Check your understanding
Open a datafile and save into a new folder

1   Open the datafile **canteen** from the folder **files_graphs** and save it into a new folder called **grc** using the filename **sales**.

2   Keep the file open.

Viewing a datafile and identifying data for a chart

Before you create a chart, you should look at the data in the datafile. Check to see:

○ *which cells you will need to select for the chart*

○ *if the data is presented in columns or rows*

○ *if the data to be plotted on the x-axis is numeric (this will affect how you define the data series for bar charts and line graphs).*

What does it mean?

Data series
The range of values that make up one set of data on a chart.

Look at the datafile **Lunch sales** in Figure 2.101.

	A	B	C	D	E	F	G
1	Lunch sales for the week						
2							
3	Item	Monday	Tuesday	Wednesday	Thursday	Friday	
4	Sandwiches	40	45	55	40	35	
5	Crisps	55	55	68	38	40	
6	Salads	21	17	25	20	25	
7	Soups	15	19	22	19	18	
8	Hot Drinks	9	11	16	16	12	
9	Cold Drinks	15	22	19	22	19	
10	Desserts	11	16	19	19	21	
11							

FIGURE 2.101 The datafile Lunch sales

- To create a **chart** to show the week's sandwich sales you would select data in **rows**.
- To create a **pie chart**, the range of cells would be **B3** to **F4**.
- To create a **bar chart** or **line graph**, the row labels in column **A** should also be selected, as Excel will use these for the titles and labels. The range of cells would be **A3** to **F4**.
- The **data labels** would be taken from row **3: Monday, Tuesday, Wednesday,** etc., and the values would be taken from row **4: 40, 45, 55,** etc.
- To create a **comparative bar** or **line graph** to show the week's sandwich and crisps sales, the range of cells would be **A3** to **F5**.

Look at the datafile **Lunch sales** in Figure 2.102.

	A	B	C	D	E	F	G
1	Lunch sales for the week						
2							
3	Item	Monday	Tuesday	Wednesday	Thursday	Friday	
4	Sandwiches	40	45	55	40	35	
5	Crisps	55	55	68	38	40	
6	Salads	21	17	25	20	25	
7	Soups	15	19	22	19	18	
8	Hot Drinks	9	11	16	16	12	
9	Cold Drinks	15	22	19	22	19	
10	Desserts	11	16	19	19	21	
11							

FIGURE 2.102 The datafile Lunch sales

- To create a **chart** to show the sales of each Item for Monday, you would select data in **columns**.
- To create a **pie chart**, the range of cells would be **A4** to **B10**. However, selecting cells **A3** to **B10** would also enable the creation of the chart.

- To create a **bar chart** or **line graph**, the column labels in row **3** should also be selected, as Excel will use these for the titles and labels. The range of cells would be **A3** to **B10**.

- The **data labels** would be taken from column **A**: *Sandwiches, Crisps, Salads*, etc., and the **values** would be taken from column **B**: *40, 55, 21*, etc.

- To create a **comparative bar or line graph** to show the Item sales for **Monday** and **Tuesday**, the range of cells would be **A3** to **C10**.

What does it mean?

Adjacent: cells that are next to each other.

▶▶ How to... *highlight a range of adjacent cells (select data)*

Method 1

1 In your datafile, click in the first cell. When the white cross displays in the cell, drag the mouse across the range (block) of cells to be highlighted.

2 A block of cells will be highlighted.

Method 2

1 Click with the mouse in the first cell.

2 Hold down the **Shift** key.

3 Click in the last cell.

4 A range (block) of cells will be highlighted.

TIP!

The first cell in a highlighted range will remain white on-screen.

TIP!

Do NOT highlight any extra cells, including any blank cells as this will affect your chart! If your selection is incorrect, click in a blank cell to deselect the data and start again.

Check your understanding
View the data in a datafile and select data

1 In your file **sales**, view the data in the rows and columns so that you are familiar with the data.

2 Highlight the data in rows from cells **B3** to **F4**.

3 Click in a blank cell to remove the highlight (to deselect the range).

4 Highlight the data in rows from cells **A3** to **F5**.

5 Click in a blank cell to remove the highlight (to deselect the range).

6 Highlight the data in columns from cells **A3** to **C10**.

7 Click in a blank cell to remove the highlight (to deselect the range).

8 Highlight the data in columns from cells **A4** to **B10**.

9 Keep this range of cells highlighted, do not deselect the range.

Using the Chart Wizard

There are several ways to create graphs in Excel. Using the Chart Wizard makes creating graphs easier because it helps you create a graph using a step-by-step approach as follows.

Step 1: Select the chart type and sub-type.

Step 2: Select or check the range of cells, preview the chart.

Step 3: Select and enter or display the chart options, e.g. Titles, Legends, Data labels.

Step 4: Select the chart location e.g. **As a new sheet**.

Pie charts

A pie chart shows data as slices of a pie. The size of each slice represents the value (number) from the data on which the chart is based – a slice shows each item of data in proportion to the whole set of data. Pie charts always show only one data series and are useful if you want to emphasise a significant element. Each slice is called a **sector**.

In Excel, there are many different pie chart sub-types. Some examples are shown in Figures 2.103, 2.104 and 2.105.

It is recommended that you always use 2-dimensional (2D) pie charts.

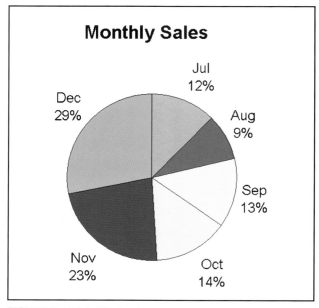

FIGURE 2.103 A 2D pie chart

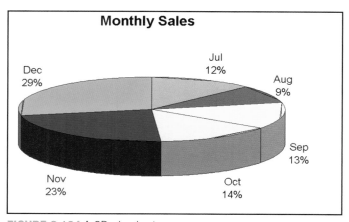

FIGURE 2.104 A 3D pie chart

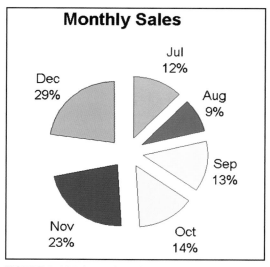

FIGURE 2.105 An exploded pie chart

The parts of a pie chart are shown in Figure 2.106.

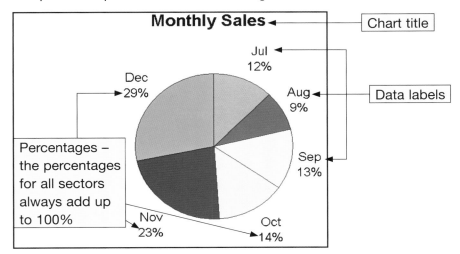

FIGURE 2.106 The parts of a pie chart

▶▶ How to...   *create a pie chart*

1   In your datafile, highlight only the relevant range of cells.

2   Click on the **Chart Wizard** 📊 icon in the Standard toolbar.

3   The **Chart Wizard – Step 1 of 4** dialogue box opens.

4   In the **Standard Types** tab, in the **Chart type** section, click on **Pie**.

5   In the **Chart sub-type** section, check that **Pie** is selected (darker) (Figure 2.107). (The box below the **Chart sub-type** describes the type of chart.)

6   Click on **Next**.

7   The **Chart Wizard – Step 2 of 4** dialogue box opens (Figure 2.108).

8   A preview of the chart is displayed.

TIP!

Numbers may be displayed for each sector instead of percentages.

TIP!

Do not highlight any extra cells or blank cells.

TIP!

If the preview of data range is incorrect, click on Cancel and start again.

FIGURE 2.107 Chart Wizard – Step 1 of 4

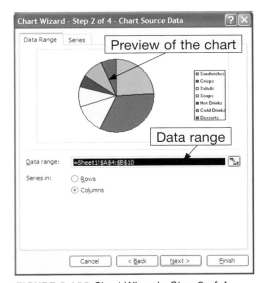

FIGURE 2.108 Chart Wizard – Step 2 of 4

9 The data range displays the selected range with the Sheet name and a $ sign before the column letter and row number.

10 You do not need to make any changes at Step 2.

11 Click on **Next**.

12 The **Chart Wizard–Step 3 of 4** dialogue box opens.

13 You will need to set options in each of the three tabs **Titles, Legend, Data Labels**.

14 Click on the **Titles** tab (Figure 2.109).

15 In the **Chart title** box, enter the title.

16 Click on the **Legend** tab (Figure 2.110).

17 Click to remove the tick in the **Show legend** box (unless required for your chart).

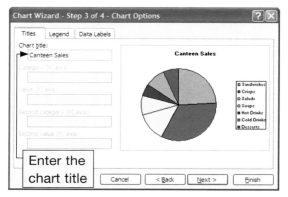

FIGURE 2.109 Chart Wizard–Step 3 of 4 in Titles view

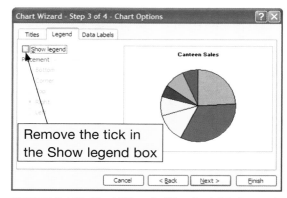

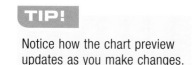

FIGURE 2.110 Chart Wizard–Step 3 of 4 in Legend view

18 Click on the **Data Labels** tab (Figure 2.111).

   a Click to insert a tick in the **Category name** box (for data labels).

   b Click to insert a tick in the **Value** or **Percentage** box (as required for your chart).

   c Click to remove the tick for **Show leader lines** (optional).

19 Click on **Next**.

> **TIP!**
>
> Notice how the chart preview updates as you make changes.

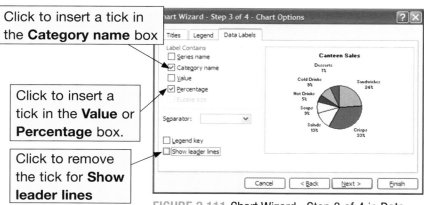

FIGURE 2.111 Chart Wizard–Step 3 of 4 in Data Labels view

20 The **Chart Wizard–Step 4 of 4** dialogue box opens (Figure 2.112).

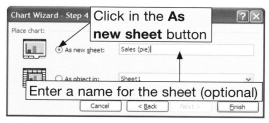

FIGURE 2.112 Chart Wizard–Step 4 of 4

21 Click in the button for **As new sheet**.

22 Enter a name for the sheet (optional).

23 Click on **Finish**.

24 The pie chart is displayed on a full page.

25 Hover with the mouse on the different parts of the chart: title, data labels, chart area, sectors. When you hover over the different areas a **Tool tip** displays showing the name of each part.

▶▶ How to... *save the updated file*

1 Click on **File** in the **Menu bar**.

2 From the menu, click on **Save**.

> **TIP!**
>
> If you have mistakenly created the chart on the spreadsheet move it to a separate sheet. Right-click within the chart in the worksheet, a menu displays, select **Location** from the menu, a **Chart Location** dialogue box displays, click the button for **As new sheet** and click **OK**.

> **TIP!**
>
> If you have made an error in the title, click on the title once you have created the chart, then click again to display the cursor and amend the title.

> **TIP!**
>
> Click on the Save icon on the Standard toolbar.

Check your understanding *Create a pie chart*

1 In your file **sales**, check that cells **A4** to **B10** are still highlighted.

2 Use the Chart Wizard to create a pie chart.

3 Enter the chart title **Canteen Sales**.

4 Do not display a legend.

5 Display **data labels** (category name) and **percentages** for each sector.

6 Make sure that you create the chart as a new sheet.

7 In the footer, add your **name**, **centre number**, an **automatic date** and an **automatic filename**.

8 Save your chart keeping the filename **sales**.

> **TIP!**
>
> 'How to... add a header or footer' and 'How to... add an automatic date and an automatic filename' were covered in Unit 2 Chapter 1 Creating Spreadsheets. If you need to revise these skills, refer to pages 20 and 21.

▶▶ How to... *print a chart*

Click on the **Print Preview** icon in the Standard toolbar.

Method 1

1 The **Print Preview** window opens.

2 Click on Print... .

3 The **Print** dialogue box is displayed.

4 Click on **OK**.

Method 2

1 The **Print Preview** window opens.

2 Close **Print Preview**.

3 The **Chart** view is displayed.

4 Click on the **Print** 🖨 icon in the **Standard toolbar**.

TIP!

Always use Print Preview to check the chart, including headers and footers, before you print.

Check your understanding *Print a pie chart*

1 Print the pie chart in your file **sales**.

2 Check your printout against the solution which can be found on the CD-ROM in the folder **graphs_worked_copies**.

Legends

A legend acts as a key for the data on a chart. It is a box that identifies the colours or patterns for each item of data. Legends are mainly used on comparative charts.

A legend should only be displayed on a pie chart if the data labels are not displayed next to each sector.

What is distinctive data?

If a chart displays a legend instead of data labels, it is very important that the legend identifies the data clearly. On the screen all the sectors are different colours, so by referring to the different colour squares in the legend, the label of each sector can be identified.

If the chart is printed in colour, the legend will still identify each sector clearly. However, if it is printed in black and white, then the sector shades are grey and the corresponding shades in the legend will be shades of grey. This can often mean that some of the grey shades are not clearly different on the printout, so that it is not possible to identify the label for each sector by referring to the legend. The chart is unusable as it does not identify the data clearly.

Using patterns in pie charts

▶▶ **How to...** *fill pie chart sectors with patterns*

Note: This is not necessary for pie charts with data labels next to the sectors.

1. In your pie chart, click on a sector. All the sectors become selected, a dot is displayed on each sector.

2. Click again to select a single sector only.

3. Make sure square handles display on one sector only.

4. Right-click to display a menu.

5. From this menu, click on **Format Data Point**.

6. A **Format Data Point** dialogue box is displayed.

7. Click on **Fill Effects**.

8. A **Fill Effects** dialogue box appears.

9. Click on the **Pattern** tab and then select a pattern.

10. To change the colour, click on the **drop-down arrow** for Foreground or Background colour, and then select a colour.

11. Click on **OK**.

12. Click on **OK** again.

Alternatively, double-click in the selected sector to open the **Format Data Point** dialogue box.

▶▶ How to... *set the option to print in black and white (to make a legend distinctive)*

1. From the **Chart** view, click on the **Print Preview** 🔍 icon to open the **Print Preview** window.

2. From **Print Preview**, click on the Setup... button in the toolbar.

3. A **Page Setup** dialogue box is displayed.

4. Click on the **Chart** tab (Figure 2.113).

5. In **Chart** view, in the **Printing quality** section, click in the **Print in black and white** box to insert a tick.

6. Click on **OK**.

7. The sectors are filled with different patterns.

8. Click on **Close** to close the **Print Preview** window.

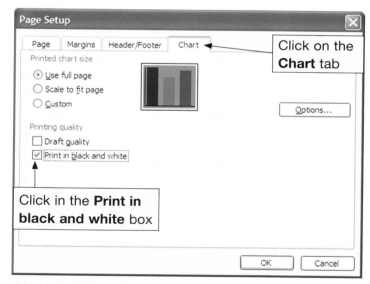

FIGURE 2.113 Page Setup box in Chart view

TIP!

Normally, for pie charts with no legend, you do not need to set the option to print in black and white.

TIP!

In the Chart view, the black and white patterns that were set will not display on-screen, but they will show on the printout.

1 In the file **sales**, set the chart to **Print in black and white**.

2 Print the chart.

3 Compare this printout to the previous one of the pie chart.

You do not need to save the updated chart.

ASSESS YOUR SKILLS – Create a pie chart

By working through Section 1 you will have learnt the skills below. Read each item to help you decide how confident you feel about each skill.

- understand pie charts
- open a provided datafile
- save the datafile using a different filename
- view the datafile and identify the data for the chart
- identify the parts of a pie chart
- select the data for a pie chart
- use the Chart Wizard to create a pie chart
- add the chart title
- show/remove the legend
- display data labels, values, percentages
- select the chart location
- save the updated file
- print the chart
- understand legends
- understand what distinctive data is and its importance
- set the chart to print in black and white to make sure that data is clearly distinctive
- fill pie chart sectors with patterns
- make sure the data is clearly distinctive on the print.

If you think you need more practice on any of the skills above, go back and work through the skill(s) again.

If you feel confident, move on to Section 2.

2: Create a bar chart and a comparative bar chart

LEARNING OUTCOMES

In this section you will learn how to:

○ understand bar charts including comparative bar charts

○ identify the parts of a bar chart

○ understand the selection of data for bar charts

○ select the data for bar charts

○ use the Chart Wizard to create a bar chart

○ enter the chart title, *x*-axis and *y*-axis titles

○ set the *y*-axis scale

○ change the fill of the plot area

○ create a comparative bar chart

○ use fill effects.

Bar charts

A bar chart is used to show data changes over a period of time, comparisons between individual items or comparisons between data. A comparative bar chart displays comparisons for two or more sets of data. Data can be displayed as vertical or horizontal bars. Excel refers to a horizontal bar chart as a bar chart and a vertical (upright) bar chart as a column chart. In the UK, bar charts are usually vertical with upright bars, so the column chart option in Excel should always be selected.

In Excel, there are many different bar chart sub-types. Some examples are shown in Figures 2.114 and 2.115.

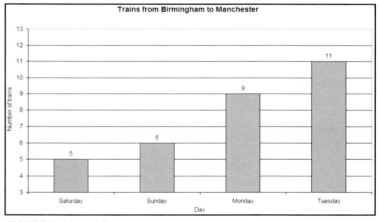

FIGURE 2.114 A 2D bar chart

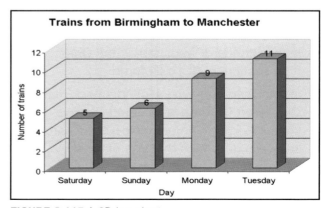

FIGURE 2.115 A 3D bar chart

It is recommended that you always use 2-dimensional vertical bar charts.

The parts of a bar chart are shown in Figure 2.116.

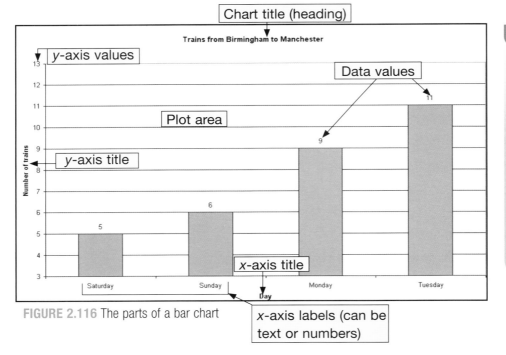

FIGURE 2.116 The parts of a bar chart

What does it mean?

x-axis labels
The *x*-axis labels are the category labels. They describe what each bar represents.

y-axis labels
The *y*-axis is the value axis. It shows the numeric value (quantity) for each bar.

Data values
Data values are the actual numbers for each data item (bar).

Before you create a bar chart, look at the data in the datafile. If the data series is numeric, at **Step 2 of 4** the **Chart** preview will be incorrect. Refer to 'How to... define the data series' on pages 91–93.

When selecting data for a bar chart, you should select the row/column labels, as Excel will use these for titles or legends.

TIP!

Do not highlight a single blank or additional cell. If you do, click in a blank cell and select the data again.

▶▶ How to... *create a bar chart*

1 In your datafile, highlight only the relevant range of cells.

2 Click on the Chart Wizard 📊 icon on the **Standard toolbar**.

3 The Chart Wizard – **Step 1 of 4** dialogue box opens (Figure 2.117).

4 In the Standard Types tab, in the Chart type section, click on **Column**.

5 In the Chart sub-type section, check that **Clustered Column** is selected (darker) (Figure 2.117). (The box below the Chart sub-type describes the type of chart.)

6 Click on Next.

TIP!

Do NOT click on **Bar**.

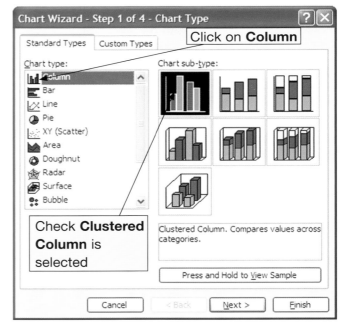

FIGURE 2.117 Chart Wizard – Step 1 of 4

7 The Chart Wizard – Step 2 of 4 dialogue box opens (Figure 2.118).

8 A preview of the chart is displayed. Check the preview.

9 Click on **Next.**

10 The **Chart Wizard – Step 3 of 4** dialogue box opens (Figure 2.119).

TIP!

If the selected data is numeric, refer to 'How to... define the data series' on pages 91–93.

11 You will need to set options in three tabs: **Titles, Legend, Data Labels**.

12 Click on the **Titles** tab (Figure 2.119).

   a In the **Chart title** box, enter the title.

   b In the **Category (X) axis** box, enter the x-axis title.

   c In the **Value (Y) axis** box, enter the y-axis title.

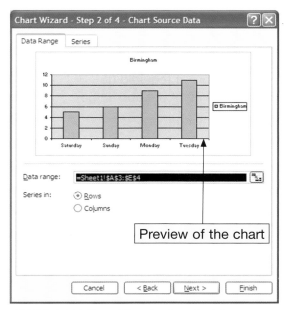

FIGURE 2.118 Chart Wizard – Step 2 of 4

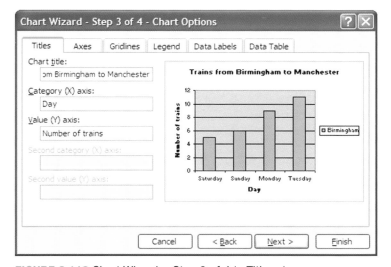

FIGURE 2.119 Chart Wizard – Step 3 of 4 in Titles view

13 Click on the **Legend** tab (Figure 2.120).

14 Click to remove the tick in the **Show legend** box if your chart is not comparative.

TIP!

Notice how the chart preview updates as you make changes.

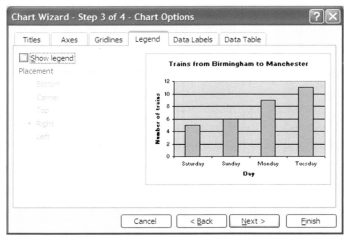

FIGURE 2.120 Chart Wizard – Step 3 of 4 in Legend view

15 Click on the **Data Labels** tab (Figure 2.121).

16 Click to insert a tick in the **Value** box if required (to display numbers above the bars).

17 Click on **Next**.

18 The **Chart Wizard – Step 4 of 4** dialogue box opens (Figure 2.122).

19 Click in the button for **As new sheet**.

20 Enter a name for the sheet (optional).

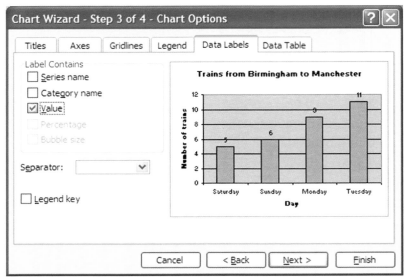

FIGURE 2.121 Chart Wizard – Step 3 of 4 in Data Labels view

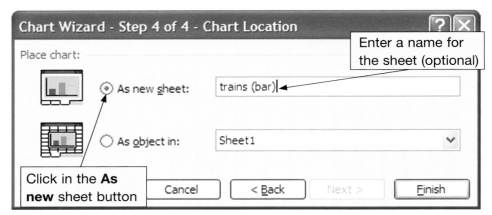

FIGURE 2.122 Chart Wizard – Step 4 of 4

21 Click on **Finish**.

22 The bar chart is displayed on a full page.

23 Hover with the mouse on the different parts of the chart: title, data labels, y-axis, y-axis title, x-axis, x-axis title, chart area, plot area, bars. A **Tool tip** displays showing the name of each part when you hover over each area of the chart.

The y-axis scale

The scale is the minimum (lowest) value and the maximum (largest) value displayed on the y-axis. Excel sets the scale that it thinks is the most appropriate for the data, however, you can change these.

▶▶ How to... *set the scale on the* y-*axis*

1 In your chart, hover with the mouse on any of the y-axis values (numbers).

2 A Value Axis **Tool tip** is displayed.

TIP!

If you have mistakenly created the chart on the spreadsheet, to move it to a separate sheet: right-click within the chart in the worksheet, a menu displays, select Location from the menu, a Chart Location window displays, click the button for As new sheet and click OK.

TIP!

If you have made an error in the title, x-axis label or y-axis label, click twice in the title or label and amend the data.

TIP!

Changes to the axis are made once the chart is created.

3 Double-click with the mouse.

4 A **Format Axis** dialogue box is displayed.

5 Click on the **Scale** tab (Figure 2.123).

6 In the **Auto** section, click in **Minimum** box.

7 Delete any numbers, then enter the required minimum value.

8 Click in the **Maximum** box.

9 Delete any numbers, then enter the required maximum value.

10 Click on **OK**.

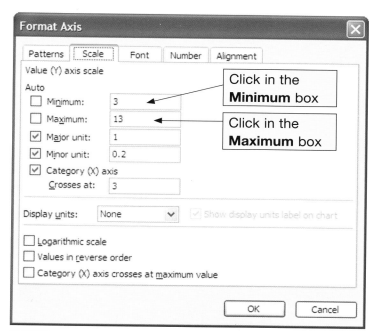

FIGURE 2.123 **Format Axis** dialogue box in **Scale** view

TIP!

When you enter minimum and maximum values, the tick in each (left-hand) box is removed, which ensures that the values remain set. If the values you are required to set are already displayed, you must click to remove the tick in the minimum/maximum box or Excel may change the value(s).

Changing the fill of the plot area

Excel displays the background of the chart (the plot area) as grey. To make the chart clearer and to save printer ink, the grey shade can be removed.

TIP!

Alternatively, double-click in the plot area to open the **Format Plot Area** dialogue box.

▶▶ **How to...** *change the fill of the plot area (optional)*

1 Hover with the mouse anywhere in the grey plot area.

2 A `Plot Area` **Tool tip** is displayed.

3 Right-click with the mouse in the plot area.

4 A menu is displayed.

5 Click on **Format Plot Area** (Figure 2.124).

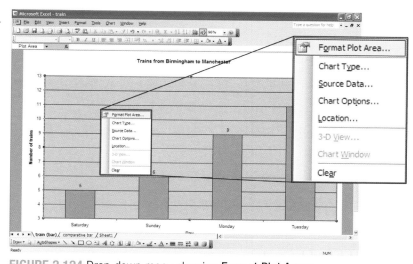

FIGURE 2.124 Drop-down menu showing **Format Plot Areas**

6   The **Format Plot Area** dialogue box displays (Figure 2.125).

7   In the **Area** section, click on **None**.

8   Click on **OK**.

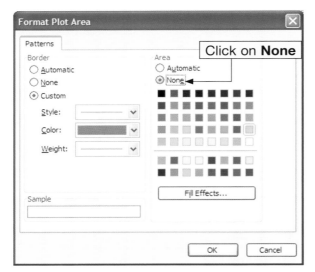

FIGURE 2.125 Format Plot Area dialogue box

TIP!

If you wish, you could select white instead of **None**.

Check your understanding   *Create a bar chart*

1   Open the datafile **birm**.

2   Save the file using the new filename **train** into the folder you created earlier called **grc**.

3   Create a bar chart to show the Trains to Manchester for **Birmingham** from **Saturday to Tuesday** only.

4   Display the day along the *x*-axis.

5   Title the chart **Trains from Birmingham to Manchester**.

6   Give the *x*-axis the title **Day**.

7   Give the *y*-axis the title **Number of trains**.

8   Do not display a legend.

9   Display data values (numbers) for each bar.

10 Make sure that the chart is created on a separate sheet.

11 Set the *y*-axis range from **3** to **13**.

12 In the footer, enter your **name**, **centre number**, an **automatic date** and an **automatic filename**.

13 Save the file keeping the filename **train.**

14 Print one copy of the bar chart.

15 Check your printout against the solution which can be found on the CD-ROM in the folder **graphs_worked_copies**.

Understanding comparative charts

Comparative charts are a simple and effective way to show a direct comparison between data in visual form.

Selecting data for comparative charts

Comparative bar charts are created in exactly the same way as simple bar charts, except that more than one data series is selected. Remember to select the row/column labels, as Excel will use these for the legend.

Legends in comparative charts

Any comparative chart MUST display a legend which should identify the data clearly on a printout. The small boxes in the legend are used to identify each set of bars.

One way of making sure that the legend identifies the data clearly is to set the option to print in black and white (described on page 77). Another method is to use a pattern fill (for the bars on bar charts or sectors on pie charts).

▶▶ How to... *use a pattern fill for bars*

1 In your chart, click on one of the bars.

2 A square dot displays in all the bars for that series (Figure 2.126).

3 Right-click in any of the bars with the dot.

4 A menu is displayed.

5 Click on **Format Data Series** (Figure 2.127).

TIP!

In the Chart Wizard – Step 2 of 4, if the preview shows the legend as Series1, Series2, this means that you have not selected the row/column labels. Refer to page 94 for How to... select the name to be displayed on the legend.

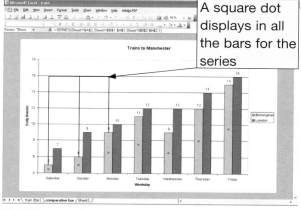

A square dot displays in all the bars for the series

FIGURE 2.126 Comparative bar chart

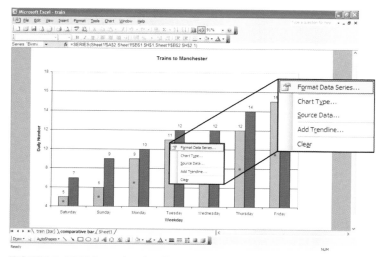

FIGURE 2.127 Menu showing Format Data Series

TIP!

Fill effects are applied after the chart is created.

TIP!

Alternatively, double-click on a bar to open the **Format Data Series** dialogue box.

6   The **Format Data Series** dialogue box appears.

7   Click on the **Patterns** tab (Figure 2.128).

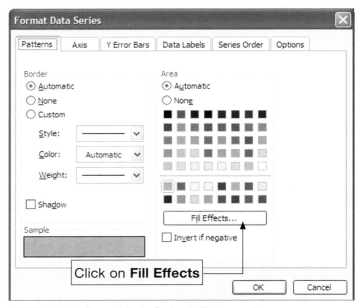

FIGURE 2.128 Format Data Series in Patterns view

8   Click on **Fill Effects**.

9   The **Fill Effects** dialogue box is displayed.

10 Click on the **Pattern** tab (Figure 2.129).

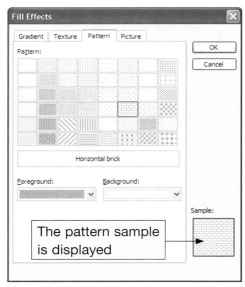

TIP!

Click on the drop-down arrow next to the Foreground and/or Background box to choose another colour.

FIGURE 2.129 Fill effects dialogue box in Pattern view

11 Click on one of the patterns in the **Pattern** section.

12 The pattern sample is displayed.

13 Click on **OK**.

14 Click on **OK** to close the
Format Data Series dialogue box.

Viewing the spreadsheet

 *view the*
spreadsheet

1 At the bottom left of the screen,
click on the sheet tab, e.g. **Sheet1**
(Figure 2.130).

2 To view the chart, click on the
chart tab.

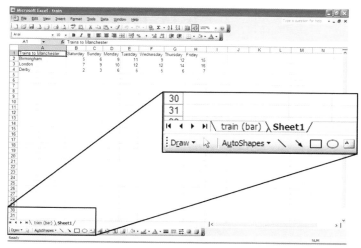

FIGURE 2.130 Sheet tab

TIP!

The chart tab in your file
may be named **Chart1**.

Check your understanding *Create a comparative bar chart*

1 In your file **train**, click on the **Sheet1** tab to see the spreadsheet.

2 Create a comparative bar chart to show the Trains to Manchester for **Birmingham** and
London from **Saturday to Friday**.

3 Display the days along the *x*-axis.

4 Title the chart **Trains to Manchester**

5 Give the *x*-axis the title **Weekday**

6 Give the *y*-axis the title **Daily Number**

7 Use a legend to identify the bars. Make sure that the bars are distinctive and can be
clearly identified when printed.

8 Display data values (numbers) for each bar.

9 Make sure that the chart is created on a separate sheet.

10 Set the *y*-axis range from **4** to **18**

11 Use a pattern fill for one data series (set of bars).

12 Enter your **name**, **centre number**, an **automatic date** and an **automatic filename** in
the header or footer.

13 Save the file keeping the filename **train**.

14 Print one copy of the comparative bar chart.

15 Make sure that the legend identifies the data clearly on the printout.

16 Close the file.

ASSESS YOUR SKILLS – Create bar a chart and a comparative bar chart

By working through Section 2 you will have learnt the skill listed below. Read each item to help you decide how confident you feel about each skill.

- understand bar charts including comparative bar charts
- identify the parts of a bar chart
- select the data for the chart
- use the Chart Wizard to create a bar chart
- add the chart title
- add the x-axis and y-axis titles
- show/remove the legend
- display data values (numbers) for the bars
- select the chart location
- set the y-axis minimum and maximum values
- change the fill of the plot area
- create a comparative bar chart
- use a pattern fill for the bars
- save the updated file
- print the chart
- close an updated file
- make sure the legend identifies the data clearly on the printout.

If you think you need more practice on any of the skills above, go back and work through the skill(s) again.

If you feel confident, move on to Section 3.

LEARNING OUTCOMES

In this section you will learn how to:

- understand line graphs
- identify the parts of a line graph
- understand the selection of data for line graphs
- select data for the graph
- use the Chart Wizard to create a line graph
- create a comparative line graph
- define the data series for numeric data
- format lines and markers.

Line graphs

Line graphs are used to show trends in data at intervals. They display a set of related values plotted as a line. A marker is usually displayed for each value (data point). Comparative line graphs show trends for more than one data series.

In Excel, there are many different line graph sub-types. Some examples are shown in Figures 2.131 and 2.132.

It is recommended that you always use 2-dimensional line graphs.

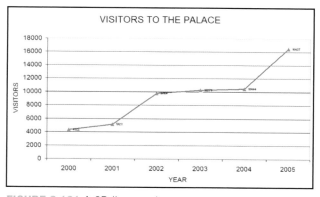

FIGURE 2.131 A 2D line graph

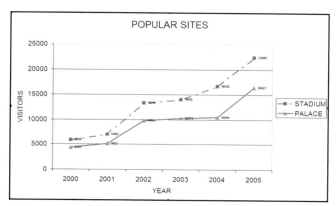

FIGURE 2.132 A 2D comparative line graph with legend

The parts of a line graph are shown in Figure 2.133.

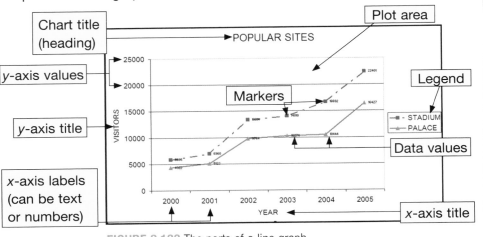

FIGURE 2.133 The parts of a line graph

What does it mean?

x-axis labels
The x-axis labels are the category labels. They describe what each data point on the line represents.

y-axis labels
The y-axis is the value axis. It shows the numeric value (quantity) for each point on the line.

Data values
Data values are the actual numbers for each data point.

Before you create a line graph, look at the data in the datafile. If the data to be plotted on the x-axis is numeric, at Step 2 of 4 the Chart preview will be incorrect. Refer to 'How to... define the data series' on page 91.

Remember, when selecting data for a line graph, you should select the row/column labels as Excel will use these for titles or legends.

▶▶ How to... *create a line graph*

1 In your datafile, highlight only the relevant range of cells.

2 Click on the **Chart Wizard** icon.

3 The **Chart Wizard – Step 1 of 4** dialogue box opens.

4 In the **Standard Types** tab, in the **Chart type** section, click on **Line**.

5 In the **Chart sub-type** section, check that the **Line with markers ...** type is selected (darker) (Figure 2.134). (The box below the **Chart sub-type** describes the type of chart.)

6 Click on **Next**.

7 The **Chart Wizard – Step 2 of 4** dialogue box opens.

8 A preview of the chart is displayed. Check the preview.

9 If the preview is correct, click on **Next** and follow the **Chart Wizard – Step 3 of 4**.

TIP!

Do not highlight any blank or additional cells. If you do, click on a blank cell to deselect the data and select the correct range of cells.

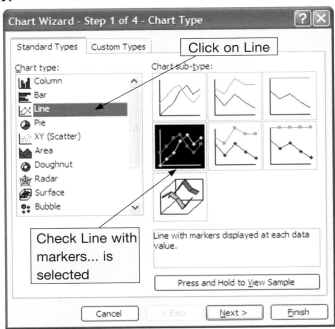

FIGURE 2.134 Chart Wizard – Step 1 of 4

10 If the preview is incorrect (e.g. it shows two lines instead of one for a simple line graph, or three lines instead of two for a comparative line graph), you MUST define the data series before continuing. Refer to 'How to... define the data series' below before going to the **Chart Wizard – Step 3 of 4**.

11 **The Chart Wizard – Step 3 of 4** dialogue box opens:

   a Enter the chart title, *x*-axis title and *y*-axis title.

   b Display/remove the legend as required.

   c Display data labels as required.

12 Click on **Next.**

13 The **Chart Wizard – Step 4 of 4** dialogue box opens.

14 Click in the button for **As new sheet.**

15 Enter a name for the sheet (optional).

16 Click on **Finish**.

17 The line graph is displayed on a full page.

Defining the data series

It may be necessary to define the data series for bar charts and line graphs. If the data to be plotted on the *x*-axis is numeric, you must check the preview of the chart in the **Chart Wizard – Step 2 of 4**. You will need to define each data series so that Excel knows which row/column of data is to be used for the *x*-axis and which should be used for the *y*-axis.

 How to... *define the data series (Chart Wizard – Step 2 of 4)*

1 In the **Chart Wizard – Step 2 of 4**, click on the **Series** tab.

2 In the **Series** section, click on the name of the series that should not be plotted on the *x*-axis (Figure 2.135).

3 Click on **Remove**.

4 The chart preview will change – the incorrect data set will be removed from the preview.

TIP!

If the data selected for the *x*-axis is numeric, Excel displays it as an additional line.

TIP!

If you have mistakenly created the chart on the spreadsheet, to move it to a separate sheet: right-click within the chart in the worksheet, a menu displays, select **Location** from the menu, a **Chart Location** window displays, click the button for **As new sheet** and click **OK**.

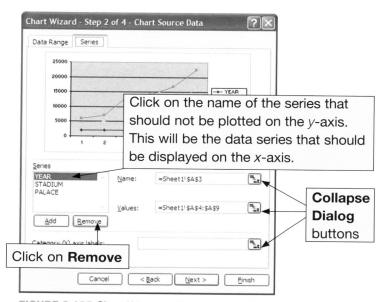

FIGURE 2.135 Chart Wizard – Step 2 of 4 in Series view

5 Click on the **Collapse Dialog** button next to **Category (X) axis labels** box.

6 You will see the spreadsheet and a small (collapsed) window (Figure 2.136)

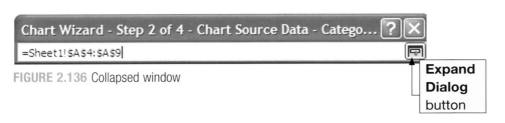

FIGURE 2.136 Collapsed window

Expand Dialog button

TIP!

Click and drag the title bar (usually blue) of the collapsed window to move it out of the way if required.

7 In the spreadsheet, highlight only the cells that should display as the *x*-axis labels. Do not include the row/column label.

8 A marquee (dotted line) displays around the selected cells (Figure 2.137).

9 The range of cells is displayed in the **Category (X) axis labels** collapsed box.

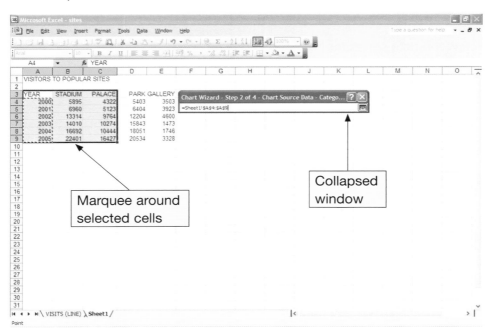

Marquee around selected cells

Collapsed window

FIGURE 2.137 Highlighted cells in spreadsheet

10 In the collapsed window, click on the **Expand Dialog** button.

11 You will be returned to the **Source Data** dialogue box.

12 Click on the **Collapse Dialog** button next to the **Values** box.

13 Highlight the correct range of cells to be plotted on the *y*-axis (do NOT include the row/column label). This may have a marquee, but it is best to define the range again.

14 In the collapsed window, click on the **Expand Dialog** button.

15 You will be returned to the **Source Data** dialogue box.

16 If you are creating a comparative chart:

   a Click on the name on the second data series (Figure 2.138).

   b Click on the **Collapse Dialog** button next to the **Values** box.

   c Highlight the correct range of cells to be plotted on the *y*-axis.

   d Click on the **Expand Dialog** button.

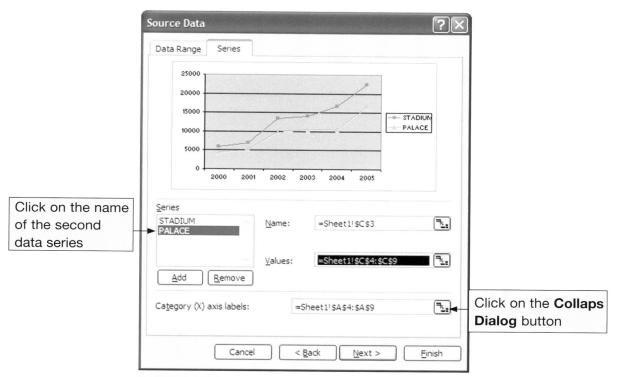

FIGURE 2.138 Second data series

17 You will be returned to the **Source Data** dialogue box.

18 In the **Source Data** dialogue box, check that the chart preview is correct. If the legend displays Series1, Series2, refer to the section Legend labels.

19 Click on **Next.**

20 Continue setting the options in Steps 3 and 4 of the Chart Wizard.

Legend labels

If the chart preview displays the legend items as Series1 and Series2, the chart is unusable. You must ensure that the legend labels identify the lines/bars in the chart correctly.

How to... *select the names to be displayed in the legend (Chart Wizard – Step 2 of 4)*

1 In the **Series** section, click on the name displayed (e.g. this may be displayed as **Series1**).

2 In the Name section, click on the **Collapse Dialog** button.

3 You will see the worksheet and a small (collapsed) window.

4 Click in the cell to be used as the name of the legend item.

5 Click the **Expand Dialog** button.

6 Repeat this process for the next legend item.

Formatting lines and markers on a line graph

On a comparative line graph, it is important that the data will be clearly distinctive on the printout if printed on a black and white printer. To make the data distinctive, the line and/or marker style may be changed.

How to... *format a line on a line graph*

1 Hover the mouse pointer over the first line on the graph.

2 Right-click with the mouse on the line.

3 A menu is displayed.

4 From the menu, select **Format Data Series**.

5 The **Format Data Series** dialogue box is displayed.

6 Click on the **Patterns** tab (Figure 2.139).

7 In the **Line** section, click in the **Custom** button.

8 To select a line style, click on the **down arrow** next to the **Style** box.

Click in the Custom button

Change the line colour

Change the line weight

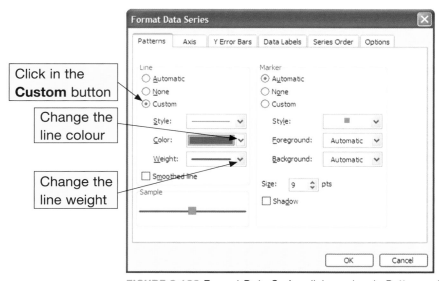

FIGURE 2.139 Format Data Series dialogue box in Patterns view.

What does it mean?

Markers
A marker is the symbol, e.g. diamond, square, etc. that shows each data point.

TIP!

Move the mouse over any part of the line and double-click to open the **Format Data Series** dialogue box.

TIP!

If **Format Data Point** displays instead of **Format Data Series**, you have clicked on a marker. Left-click in the graph to deselect the marker, then hover the mouse pointer over the line and double-click to open the **Format Data Series** dialogue box.

TIP!

For comparative line graphs, choose one dotted line and one solid line.

9 To select a line weight, click on the **down arrow** next to the **Weight** box. Choose a thick line as this will be clearer on the printout.

10 Change the line colour by clicking on the down arrow next to the **Color** box (optional).

11 Click on **OK** to format the line (to format the markers, see below).

▶▶ How to... *format the markers on a line*

1 Follow steps 1–6 of 'How to... format a line on a line graph' (see above).

2 In the **Marker** section, click in the **Custom** button.

3 Click on the **down arrow** next to the **Style** box.

4 Choose one of the marker styles.

5 To change the marker colour, click on the **down arrow** next to the **Foreground** and/or **Background** box (optional).

6 Click on **OK** to format the markers.

> **TIP!**
>
> Format either the lines or the markers.

Check your understanding *Create a comparative line graph*

1 Open the datafile **tourists**.

2 Save the file using the new filename **sites** into the folder **grc**.

3 Create a comparative line graph to show the visitors to popular sites for the **YEAR** from **2000 to 2005** for **STADIUM** and **PALACE**.

4 Display the years along the *x*-axis.

5 Title the graph **POPULAR SITES**.

6 Give the *x*-axis the title **YEAR**.

7 Give the *y*-axis the title **VISITORS**.

8 Use a legend to identify each line. Make sure that the lines and/or data points are distinctive and can be clearly identified when printed.

9 Display the values (numbers) for each data point on both lines.

10 Make sure that the chart is created on a separate sheet.

11 In the footer, enter your **name**, **centre number**, an **automatic date** and an **automatic filename**.

12 Save the file keeping the filename **sites**.

13 Print one copy of the line graph.

14 Make sure that the legend clearly identifies the data on the printout.

15 Close the file.

16 Check your printout against the solution which can be found on the CD-ROM in the folder **graphs_worked_copies**.

> **TIP!**
>
> Even if there is no instruction to format the plot area to be white, it is good practice to do so.

ASSESS YOUR SKILLS – Create a line graph and a comparative line graph

By working through Section 3 you will have learnt the skills listed below. Read each item to help you decide how confident you feel about each skill.

- understand line graphs including comparative line graphs
- identify the parts of a line graph
- select the data for the graph
- use the Chart Wizard to create a line graph
- define the data series
- add the chart title
- add the x-axis and y-axis titles
- show/remove the legend
- display data values (numbers) for the lines
- select the chart location
- create a comparative line graph
- format the line(s)
- format the markers
- save the updated file
- print the chart
- close an updated file
- make sure that the legend identifies the data clearly on the printout.

If you think you need more practice on any of the skills above, go back and work through the skill(s) again.

If you feel confident, do the Build-up and Practice tasks.

Remember, you can refer to the Quick reference guides on pages 97–106 when doing any tasks and during an assessment.

QUICK REFERENCE – *Create a new spreadsheet*

Keep a copy of this page next to you. Refer to it when working through tasks and during any assessments.

HOW TO...	METHOD	QUICK METHOD
Start Excel	Click on Start → All Programs → Microsoft Office → Microsoft Office Excel 2003.	Single-click on the Excel icon on the Quick Launch bar OR double-click on the Excel icon on the desktop.
Create a new spreadsheet	Click on File menu → New (note: a new blank spreadsheet opens when you load Excel).	Click on the New icon on the toolbar.
Set orientation	Click on File menu → Page Setup → Page tab → click on Portrait or Landscape → click on OK.	
Enter data	Click in cell where data is to be entered → enter data → to move to next cell, use a Cursor key OR click with the mouse in the cell OR use the Tab key.	
Widen columns	Double-click between grey column dividers or drag ↔ to widen individual columns, OR highlight cells → click on Format menu → click on Column → click on AutoFit Selection.	Highlight the entire spreadsheet (click in top left grey cell) → double-click on ↔ in between any of the grey column letters.
Save a spreadsheet	Click on File menu → click on Save → Save As dialogue box displays → click on down arrow to right of Save in box, then click on your user area → in File name box → delete any existing text → enter required filename → click on Save.	Click on the Save icon → enter a filename → make sure you save into the correct folder → click on Save OR press Ctrl + S.
Save a spreadsheet into a new folder from within Excel	Click on File menu → click on Save → Save As dialogue box displays → click on down arrow to right of Save in box, then click on your user area → click on the Create New Folder icon → New Folder dialogue box opens → enter new folder name → click on OK → in File name box → delete any existing text → enter required filename → click on Save.	Click on the Save icon → Save As dialogue box displays → click on down arrow to right of Save in box, then click on your user area → click on the Create New Folder icon → New Folder dialogue box opens → enter new folder name → click on OK → in File name box → delete any existing text → enter required filename → click on Save. To save an existing spreadsheet with a new filename, use Save As not Save.

(continued overleaf)

HOW TO...	METHOD	QUICK METHOD
Add a header or footer	Click on View menu → click on Header and Footer → Header dialogue box displays → click in Left, Center or Right section → enter required information in Left, Center or Right section → click on OK → click on OK in Page Setup dialogue box.	Click on View menu → click on Header and Footer → Page Setup dialogue box displays → click on Custom Header → Header dialogue box displays → click in Left, Center or Right section → enter required information → click on OK → click on Custom Footer → Footer dialogue box displays → enter required information in Left, Center or Right section → click on OK → click on OK in Page Setup dialogue box.
Add an automatic date	Click on View menu → click on Header and Footer → click in Left, Center or Right section → click on Insert Date icon → click on OK → click on OK in Page Setup dialogue box.	Click on View menu → click on Header and Footer → Page Setup dialogue box displays → click on Custom Header → click in Left, Center or Right section → click on OK → click on OK in Page Setup dialogue box.
Add an automatic filename	Click on View menu → click on Header and Footer → click in Left, Center or Right section → click on Insert Filename icon → click on OK → click on OK in Page Setup dialogue box.	Click on View menu → click on Header and Footer → Page Setup dialogue box displays → click on Custom Header → click on OK → click on OK in Page Setup dialogue box.
Save an existing spreadsheet	Click on File menu → click on Save. To save with a new filename, use Save As.	Click on the Save icon OR press Ctrl + S.
Fit to one page	Click on File menu → click on Page Setup → Page Setup dialogue box displays → click on Page tab → in Scaling section → click on Fit to button → check display is 1 in page(s) wide by box and 1 in tall box.	
Print a document	Click on File menu → click on Print → Print dialogue box displays → check Page Range is set to All → set Number of copies to 1 → click on OK.	Once you have set the Print settings (e.g. orientation, fit to one page, etc.) → click on the Print icon.

click means click with the left mouse button

QUICK REFERENCE – *Edit a spreadsheet*

Keep a copy of this page next to you. Refer to it when working through tasks and during any assessments.

HOW TO...	METHOD	QUICK METHOD
Edit data	Click in the relevant cell → click in Formula bar → delete existing data → enter the new data → press Enter or click in another cell.	Double-click in the relevant cell → delete unwanted content → enter new data.
Insert a column	Click anywhere in the column where the new column is to be inserted → click on Insert menu → click on Columns → a new blank column is inserted and subsequent columns are automatically relabelled.	Right-click in the column letter where the new column is to be inserted → the entire column is highlighted and a menu displays → click on Insert.
Insert a row	Click anywhere in the row where the new row is to be inserted → click on Insert menu → click on Rows → a new blank row is inserted and subsequent rows are automatically renumbered.	Right-click in the row letter where the new row is to be inserted → the entire row is highlighted and a menu displays → click on Insert.
Delete a column	Move mouse pointer over grey column letter to be deleted and click → entire column is highlighted → right-click in highlighted column → a menu displays → click on Delete → column is deleted and remaining columns are automatically relabelled.	Move mouse pointer over grey column letter to be deleted and right-click → a menu displays → click on Delete → column is deleted and remaining columns are automatically relabelled.
Delete a row	Move mouse pointer over grey row number to be deleted and click → entire row is highlighted → right-click in highlighted row → a menu displays → click on Delete → row is deleted and remaining rows are automatically renumbered. OR, click anywhere in the row to be deleted → click on the Edit menu → click on Delete → Delete dialogue box displays → click in the button for Entire Row → click on OK.	Move mouse pointer over grey row number to be deleted and right-click → a menu displays → click on Delete → row is deleted and remaining rows are automatically renumbered.
Display formulae	Click on Tools menu → click on Options → Options dialogue box displays → click on View tab → click in Formulas box to insert tick → click on OK.	Press Ctrl + ` (Accent key above the Tab key).
Adjust column widths	Double-click with left mouse button on the vertical line in the grey area displaying the column letters dividing two columns OR drag the vertical line to make column wider until all data is displayed in full. OR, highlight the cells → click on Format menu → click on Column → click on AutoFit Selection.	Use AutoFit to adjust the column widths of all columns → click on shaded cell to left of column letter and above row number → double-click in between any of the grey column letters.

(continued overleaf)

HOW TO...	METHOD	QUICK METHOD
Display gridlines	Click on File menu → click on Page Setup → Page Setup dialogue box displays → click on Sheet tab → click in Gridlines box to insert tick → click on OK.	
Display row and column headings	Click on File menu → Page Setup dialogue box displays → click on Sheet tab → click in Row and column headings box to insert tick → click on OK.	
Format with currency symbol and set decimal places	Highlight relevant cells → right-click within highlighted cells → a menu displays → click on Format Cells → Format Cells dialogue box displays → click on Number tab → click on Currency → in Decimal places box → use up/down arrows to display required number of decimal places → in Symbol box → click on down arrow and click on required currency format, e.g. £ → click on OK.	
Format decimal places	Highlight relevant cells → right-click within highlighted cells → a menu displays → click on Format Cells → Format Cells dialogue box displays → click on Number tab → in Decimal places box → use up/down arrow to display required number of decimal places → click on OK.	
Align data	Highlight relevant cells → click on Align Left, Align Right or Center icon. OR, highlight cells → click on Format menu → click on Cells → Format Cells dialogue box displays → click on Alignment tab → click on drop-down arrow next to Horizontal → click on required alignment → click on OK.	
Add a border	Highlight relevant cells → on the toolbar → click on down arrow next to Borders icon → drop-down selection displays → click on Outside Borders or Thick Box Border option. OR, highlight cells → click on Format menu → click on Cells → Format Cells dialogue box displays → click on Border tab → click on Outline → in the Line section → click on the thick line style option → click on drop-down arrow next to Color → select black → click on OK.	
Use shading	Highlight relevant cells → on the toolbar → click on down arrow next to Fill Color icon → drop-down menu displays → select suitable colour. OR, highlight cells → click on Format menu → click on Cells → Format Cells dialogue box displays → click on Patterns tab → click on required shade (not too dark as text cannot be read and not too light as shade must show on the printout) → click on OK.	
Close a spreadsheet	Click on File menu → click on Close.	Click on black cross.
Exit from Excel	Click File menu → click on Exit.	Click on red cross.
Close a spreadsheet and exit Excel	Click on File menu → click on Close → click on File menu → click on Exit.	Click on black cross → click on red cross.

QUICK REFERENCE – Use formulae and functions in spreadsheets

Keep a copy of this page next to you. Refer to it when working through tasks and during any assessments.

HOW TO...	METHOD
Create a simple formula with + (add)	Click in cell → enter an = sign → click in cell that contains first value (number) → cell reference displays in Formula bar → enter the + sign → click in cell that contains second value → cell reference of second cell displays after + sign → check Formula bar to make sure formula is correct → press Enter key OR click on Enter tick in Formula bar.
Create a simple formula with – (subtract)	Click in cell → enter an = sign → click in cell that contains first value (number) → cell reference displays in Formula bar → enter the – sign → click in cell that contains second value → cell reference of second cell displays after – sign → check Formula bar to make sure formula is correct → press Enter key OR click on Enter tick in Formula bar.
Create a simple formula with * (multiply)	Click in cell → enter an = sign → click in cell that contains first value (number) → cell reference displays in Formula bar → enter the * sign → click in cell that contains second value → cell reference of second cell displays after * sign → check Formula bar to make sure formula is correct → press Enter key OR click on Enter tick in Formula bar.
Create a simple formula with / (divide)	Click in cell → enter an = sign → click in cell that contains first value (number) → cell reference displays in Formula bar → enter the / sign → click in cell that contains second value → cell reference of second cell displays after / sign → check Formula bar to make sure formula is correct → press Enter key OR click on Enter tick in Formula bar.
Replicate (copy) a formula	*Method 1:* Click in the cell containing the formula to be copied → click on fill handle (black square on the bottom right of the cell) → drag fill handle over the cells that formula is to be copied into. *Method 2:* Click in the cell containing the formula to be copied → click on the Edit menu → click on Copy → a marquee displays around the copied cell → highlight the cells that you want to copy the formula to → click on the Edit menu → click on Paste → press the Enter key to stop the marquee.

(continued overleaf)

HOW TO...	METHOD
Use brackets in a formula	Click in the relevant cell → enter an = sign → enter an opening bracket (→ click in cell that contains the first number → the bracket and cell reference display in the Formula bar → enter a + or - or / sign → click in cell that contains the second value → the cell reference of the second cell displays in the Formula bar after the mathematical operator → enter a closing bracket → enter a + or - or * or / sign → click in the cell that contains the third value → check the Formula bar to make sure the formula is correct → press the Enter key on keyboard OR click on the Enter tick in the Formula bar.
Use AUTOSUM	Use only for cells that are next to each other: Highlight the cells to be added and the cell in which to display the result → Click on the AutoSum icon.
Use the SUM function	Method 1: Click in the relevant cell → enter an = sign → enter the word SUM and an opening bracket (→ highlight the range of cells to be added → enter a closing bracket) → press the Enter key OR click on the Enter tick in the Formula bar.
	Method 2: Click in the relevant cell → click on the fx Insert Function icon on the Formula bar → Insert Function dialogue box displays → click on the word SUM → click on OK → Function Arguments dialogue box displays → check the range of cells in the Number 1 row → click on OK.
Use the AVERAGE function	Method 1: Click in the relevant cell → enter an = sign → enter the word AVERAGE and an opening bracket (→ highlight the range of cells to be averaged → enter a closing bracket) → press the Enter key OR click on the Enter tick in the Formula bar.
	Method 2: Click in the relevant cell → click on the fx Insert Function icon on the Formula bar → Insert Function dialogue box displays → click on the word AVERAGE → click on OK → Function Arguments dialogue box displays → check the range of cells in the Number 1 row → click on OK.

Click means click with the left mouse button

QUICK REFERENCE – Creating graphs

Keep a copy of this page next to you. Refer to it when working through tasks and during any assessments.

HOW TO...	METHOD
Start Excel	Click on Start → All Programs → Microsoft Office → Microsoft Office Excel 2003.
Open a datafile from Excel	Click on File menu → click on Open → Open dialogue box displays → click on drop-down arrow next to Look in box → find your user area and double-click on it to open → double-click on folder containing files → list of files displays → double-click on file (instead of double-click, you can single-click, then click on Open).
Open a datafile from My Computer	From desktop → double-click on My Computer icon → My Computer window opens → go to your user area → double-click to open → find folder containing files → double-click on folder to open → look for required file → double-click on file → file opens in Excel.
Save a datafile into a new folder from within Excel	Click on File menu → click on Save As → Save As dialogue box displays → click on down arrow next to Save in box, then click on your user area → click on Create New Folder icon (or, to save in existing folder, double-click on folder name) → New Folder dialogue box displays → enter new folder name → click on OK → in File name box → delete any existing text → enter required filename → click on Save.
Highlight a range of cells	*Method 1:* Click in the first cell, a white cross displays, and drag the mouse across the range (block) of cells to be highlighted. *Method 2:* Click with the mouse in the first cell → hold down the Shift key → click in the last cell.
Create a pie chart	Highlight only the relevant range of cells → click on the Chart Wizard icon → in Step 1 of 4, in Standard Types tab, in Chart type section → click on Pie → in Chart sub-type section, check that Pie is selected → click on Next → in Step 2 of 4 → check the chart preview → if preview is correct, click on Next (if incorrect, click on Cancel and start again) → in Step 3 of 4 → click on Titles tab → in Chart title box, enter the title → click on Legend tab → click to remove tick in Show legend box (unless required) → click on Data Labels tab → click in Category name box (for data labels) → click in Value or Percentage box → click to deselect Show leader lines → click on Next → In Step 4 of 4 → click button for As new sheet → click on Finish.
Set a chart to print in black and white	From chart view, click on Print Preview icon → click on Setup → in Page Setup dialogue box → click on Chart tab → click on button for Print in black and white → click on OK → click on Close (patterns will not display in chart view but will print).
Fill pie chart sectors with patterns	Click on a sector, then click again to select it → make sure square handles display on one sector only → right-click → a menu displays → click on Format Data Point → Format Data Point dialogue box displays → click on Fill Effects button → Fill Effects dialogue box displays → click on Pattern tab → select a pattern → click on OK.

(continued overleaf)

HOW TO...	METHOD
Create a bar chart	Highlight only the relevant range of cells (include row or column labels) → click on the Chart Wizard icon → in Step 1 of 4, in Standard Types tab, in Chart type section → click on Column → in Chart sub-type section, check that Clustered Column is selected → click on Next → in Step 2 of 4 → check the chart preview → if preview is correct, click on Next (if incorrect, refer to 'Define the data series (bar charts or line graphs')). → In Step 3 of 4 → click on Titles tab → in Chart Title box, enter the title → click in Category (X) axis box → enter x-axis title → click in Value (Y) axis box → enter y-axis title → click on Legend tab → click to remove tick in Show legend box → click on Data Labels tab → click in Value box (to display numbers on bars) → click on Next → in Step 4 of 4 → click in button for As new sheet → click on Finish.
Create a comparative bar chart	Highlight only the relevant range of cells (include row or column labels) → click on the Chart Wizard icon → in Step 1 of 4, in Standard Types tab, in Chart type section → click on Column → in Chart sub-type section, check that Clustered Column is selected → click on Next → in Step 2 of 4 → check the chart preview → if preview is correct, click on Next (if incorrect, refer to 'Define the data series (for comparative charts'). → In Step 3 of 4 → click on Titles tab → in Chart Title box, enter the title → click in Category (X) axis box → enter x-axis title → click in Value (Y) axis box → enter y-axis title → click on Legend tab → check for tick in Show legend box (should be ticked) → click on Data Labels tab → click in Value box (to display numbers on bars) → click on Next → in Step 4 of 4 → click in button for As new sheet → refer to 'How to... fill bars with pattern' (below).
Set the y-axis scale (bar charts or line graphs)	Hover with mouse pointer on any number on y-axis scale → Value Axis Tool tip displays → double-click with mouse → Format Axis dialogue box displays → click on Scale tab → click in Minimum box → delete existing number → enter value (number) → click in Maximum box → delete existing number → enter value → click on OK.
Format plot area (bar charts and line graphs)	Hover with mouse in grey plot area → Plot Area Tool tip displays → right-click → a menu displays → click on Format Plot Area → Format Plot Area dialogue box displays → in Area section on the right → click on None → click on OK.
Fill bars with pattern	Click on one bar → square dot displays for that series (all bars with same colour) → right-click in any bar → a menu displays → click on Format Data Series → Format Data Series dialogue box displays → click on the Patterns tab → click on Fill Effects button → Fill Effects dialogue box displays → click on Pattern tab → click on a pattern → to change colour, click on drop-down arrow next to Foreground or Background box → select colour → click on OK → click on OK to close Format Data Series dialogue box.

HOW TO...	METHOD
Create a line graph	Highlight only the relevant range of cells (include row or column labels) → click on the Chart Wizard icon → in Step 1 of 4, in Standard Types tab, in Chart type section → click on Line → in Chart sub-type section, check that Line with markers ... is selected → click on Next → in Step 2 of 4 → check the chart preview → if preview is correct, click on Next (if incorrect, refer to 'Define the data series (bar charts or line graphs)'). → In Step 3 of 4 → click on Titles tab → in Chart Title box, enter the title → click in Category (X) axis box → enter x-axis title → click in Value (Y) axis box → enter y-axis title → click on Legend tab → click to remove tick in Show legend box → click on Data Labels tab → click in Value box (to display numbers on data points) → click on Next → in Step 4 of 4 → click in button for As new sheet → click on Finish.
Create a comparative line graph	Highlight only the relevant range of cells (include row or column labels) → click on the Chart Wizard icon → in Step 1 of 4, in Standard Types tab, in Chart type section → click on Line → in Chart sub-type section, check that Line with markers ... is selected → click on Next → in Step 2 of 4 → check the chart preview → if preview is correct, click on Next (if incorrect, refer to 'Define the data series (for comparative charts')). → In Step 3 of 4 → click on Titles tab → in Chart Title box, enter the title → click in Category (X) axis box → enter x-axis title → click in Value (Y) axis box → enter y-axis title → click on Legend tab → check for tick in Show legend box (should be ticked) → click on Data Labels tab → click in Value box (to display numbers on data points) → click on Next → in Step 4 of 4 → click in button for As new sheet → click on Finish.
Define the data series (bar charts or line graphs)	In Chart Wizard – Step 2 of 4 → click on Series tab → under chart preview in Series section → click on name of series → click on Remove → next to Category (X) axis labels box, click on Collapse Dialog button → the spreadsheet displays → highlight only the cells to be plotted on the x-axis (do not include the row/column label) → dotted line (marquee) surrounds cells → click on Expand Dialog button from collapsed window → Source Data dialogue box displays → next to Values box, click on Collapse Dialog button → the spreadsheet displays → highlight only the cells to be plotted on the y-axis (do not include the row/column label) → dotted line (marquee) surrounds cells → click on Expand Dialog button from collapsed window → check that chart preview is correct → click on Next.
Define the data series for comparative charts (bar charts or line graphs)	In Chart Wizard – Step 2 of 4 → click on Series tab → under chart preview in Series section → click on name of series → click on Remove → next to Category (X) axis labels box, click on Collapse Dialog button → the spreadsheet displays → highlight only the cells to be plotted on the x-axis (do not include the row/column label) → dotted line (marquee) surrounds cells → click on Expand Dialog button from collapsed window → Source Data dialogue box displays. → *For first data series:* Next to Values box, click on Collapse Dialog button → the spreadsheet displays → highlight only the cells to be plotted on the y-axis (do not include the row/column label) → dotted line (marquee) surrounds cells → click on Expand Dialog button from collapsed window → Source Data dialogue box displays. → *For second data series:* Under chart preview in series section → click on name of second series → next to Values box, click on Collapse Dialog button → the spreadsheet displays → highlight only the cells that should be displayed on the y-axis (do not include the row/column label) → dotted line (marquee) surrounds cells → click on Expand Dialog button from collapsed window → Source Data dialogue box displays → check that chart preview is correct → click on Next.

(continued overleaf)

HOW TO...	METHOD
Select the name for legend items	In Chart Wizard – Step 2 of 4 → click on Series tab → in Series section, click on name of first series (may be displayed as Series1) → in the Name section, delete any existing text then click on the Collapse Dialog button → the spreadsheet displays → click in the cell to be used as the name of the legend item → click on Expand Dialog → click on the name of the second series (may be displayed as Series2) → repeat this process.
Format lines on a line graph	Hover with mouse on a line → right-click → a menu displays → click on Format Data Series → Format Data Series dialogue box displays → click on Patterns tab → in Line section → click on Custom button → click on down arrow next to Style box → select a style → click on down arrow next to Weight box → select a thick line → to change colour, click on drop-down arrow next to Color box* → click on OK. *To format markers, move to right section of Format Data Series dialogue box.
Format markers on a line graph	Hover with mouse pointer on a line → right-click → a menu displays → click on Format Data Series → Format Data Series dialogue box displays → click on Patterns tab → in Marker section → click on drop-down arrow next to Style box → select a style → to change marker colour, click on drop-down arrow next to Foreground and/or Background box(es) → select colour → click on OK.
Add a header or footer	Click on View menu → click on Header and Footer → Page Setup dialogue box displays → click on Custom Header → Header dialogue box displays → click in Left, Center or Right section → enter required information → click on OK → click on Custom Footer → Footer dialogue box displays → enter required information in Left, Center or Right section → click on OK → click on OK in Page Setup dialogue box.
Add an automatic date	Click on View menu → click on Header and Footer → Page Setup dialogue box displays → click on Custom Header → click in Left, Center or Right section → click on Insert Date icon → click on OK → click on OK in Page Setup dialogue box.
Add an automatic filename	Click on View menu → click on Header and Footer → Page Setup dialogue box displays → click on Custom Header → click in Left, Center or Right section → click on Insert Filename icon → click on OK → click on OK in Page Setup dialogue box.
Save an existing datafile	Click on the Save icon.
Close a datafile	Click on File menu → click on Close.
Exit from Excel	Click on File menu → click on Exit.

Scenario

You are working in the ticket office of a local cinema. You are required to produce a spreadsheet to analyse sales of the cinema's revenue.

1 a Create a new spreadsheet.
  b Set the page orientation to **landscape**.

2   Enter the following data, leaving the **Takings** and **Total** columns blank as shown.

Cinema Takings						
Day	Five Ways	Ticket Price	Takings	Expenses	Refreshments	Total
Monday	200	3.5		54	35	
Wednesday	250	3.75		66	42	
Friday	400	4.2		76	88	
Saturday	450	4.75		85	92	
Sunday	175	4.5		65	78	
Week Total						

You need to make some calculations in your spreadsheet.

3 a In the **Takings** column use a formula to calculate the Takings for Monday by multiplying the **Five Ways** figure by the **Ticket Price**.
  b Replicate (copy) this formula to show the **Takings** for all other Days.

4 a In the **Total** column use a formula to calculate the Total for Monday as follows: (**Takings** subtract **Expenses**) plus **Refreshments**.
  b Replicate (copy) this formula for all other Days.

5   Save the spreadsheet using the filename **cinema1**.

In your saved file **cinema1**:

6 a In the **Week Total** row, use the **SUM** function to calculate the total for **Five Ways** from **Monday** to **Sunday**.
  b Replicate this function for all remaining columns

7 a In the footer:
    i Enter your **name** and **centre number**.
    ii Insert an **automatic date** and an **automatic filename**.
  b Set the spreadsheet to fit on **one page**.

8   Make sure that all data is displayed in full.

9   Save the spreadsheet, keeping the filename **cinema1**.

10   Print one copy of the spreadsheet on **one page** in **landscape** orientation, showing the figures, not the formulae.

11   Close the spreadsheet.

You will need to make some amendments in your saved spreadsheet **cinema1** and apply some formatting. (Alternatively, you may use the file **cinema1** from the worked copies folder.)

Open your saved spreadsheet **cinema1**.

1   The cinema will no longer be opening on Mondays.
  a Delete the **Monday** row.
  b Make sure blank cells do not remain where the data was deleted.

2 a Insert a new row with the label **Thursday** between Wednesday and Friday.
  b Enter data into the Thursday row as follows:

Day	Five Ways	Ticket Price	Takings	Expenses	Refreshments	Total
Thursday	100	2.55		44	25	

3   Copy the formula for **Takings** and **Total** from the Wednesday row into the Thursday row.

4   Make sure that the formulae in the Week Total row have updated after the Monday row was deleted and the Thursday row added.

5   Save your spreadsheet using the new filename **cinema2**.

6   Apply the following alignments:
  a Centre the column label **Day**.
  b **All** other text in the first column should be displayed as left-aligned.
  c Display all numeric data as right-aligned.

7   Format the numbers as follows:
  a Display the figures in the **Ticket Price** column with a **currency symbol** and **2** decimal places.
  b Display the figures in the **Total** column with a **currency symbol** and in **integer** format (zero decimal places).
  c Display the figures in all the other columns in **integer** format (zero decimal places).

8   Add a single outside border around all the column labels starting with **Day** and ending with **Total**.

9   Save the spreadsheet keeping the filename **cinema2**.

10 Print one copy of the spreadsheet on one page.

BUILD-UP TASK ③ *Edit a spreadsheet*

You need to update your saved spreadsheet **cinema2**. (You may use the file **cinema2** from the worked copies folder.)

1 Make the following changes to the spreadsheet file **cinema2**.

   a Change the label Week Total to **Weekly Total**.
   b Change the Expenses figure for Friday to **85**.
   c Change the Ticket Price for Wednesday to **£3.25**. (The currency symbol should remain displayed.)
   d Make sure that all the figures have recalculated as a result of these changes.

2 a Save the spreadsheet using the new filename **cinema3**.
   b Make sure **gridlines** will be displayed on the printout.
   c Print one copy of the spreadsheet on **one page** in **landscape** orientation showing the **figures**, not the formulae.

3 a Display the formulae. Make sure they are displayed in full.
   b Make sure that the page orientation is **landscape** and that the spreadsheet fits on one page.
   c Make sure that **gridlines** and **row and column headings** (1, 2, 3, etc. and A, B, C, etc.) will be displayed when printed.
   d Save the spreadsheet formulae using the new filename **cinform**.
   e Print the entire spreadsheet on **one page** in **landscape** orientation showing the **formulae**.
   f Make sure that all formulae are displayed in full and are readable on your printout.
   g Close the file **cinform**.

4 Close all open files.

5 Check your printouts for accuracy.

BUILD-UP TASK ④ *Create a pie chart*

For this task, you will need the file **agent** from the folder **files_graphs**.

Scenario

You work for a letting agent who has asked you to produce a pie chart to show the flats available for rent in August 2006.

1 Using suitable software for creating graphs, open the datafile **agent** which contains data about properties available for rent.

2 a Create a pie chart to show the **Number** for all **Flat Types**.

   b Title the chart **Flats Available August 2006**.

   c Do not display a legend.

   d Display data labels and percentages for each sector.

(continued overleaf)

e Make sure that the chart is created on a full page on a sheet that is separate from the source data.

3 In the **header**, enter your **name**, **centre number**, an **automatic date** and an **automatic filename**.

4 Save the file using the filename **rent**.

5 Print one copy of the pie chart.

6 Close the file.

7 Check your printout for accuracy.

 BUILD-UP TASK 5 *Create a bar chart*

For this task, you will need the file **tickets** from the folder **files_graphs**.

Scenario

You work in a school music department which holds several concerts in an academic year. Concert tickets are sold at full or reduced price (concession tickets are available for children and senior citizens). You have been asked to produce a graph to show the concert ticket sales.

1 Using suitable software for creating graphs, open the datafile **tickets** which gives figures for the tickets sold.

2a Create a comparative bar chart to show the **Concert** tickets sold for **Full Price** and **Concession.**

b Display the **Concert** along the *x*-axis.

c Title the chart **Attendance at Concerts**.

d Give the *x*-axis the title **Concert**.

e Give the *y*-axis the title **Tickets Sold**.

f Use a legend to identify the bars. Make sure that the bars are distinctive and can be clearly identified when printed.

g Display the values (numbers) for each bar.

> **TIP!**
> You may use pattern fills.

h Make sure that the chart is created on a full page on a sheet that is separate from the source data.

i Set the *y*-axis range from **50 to 450**.

3 In the footer, enter your **name, centre number,** an **automatic date** and an **automatic filename**.

4 Save the file using the filename **concerts**.

5 Print one copy of the bar chart.

6 Close the file.

7 Check your printout for accuracy.

For this task, you will need the file **visitors** from the folder **files_graphs**.

Scenario

You work in an events organising team. You need to produce a graph to show the number of visitors to an annual exhibition.

1 Using suitable software for creating graphs, open the datafile **visitors**, which gives figures for the number of visitors to the exhibition each year.

2a Create a line graph to show the **Visitors** from **2006 to 2002** only. Do not include the data for 2001.

  b Display the **Year** along the *x*-axis.

  c Title the graph **Art in Action**.

  d Give the *x*-axis the title **Year**.

  e Give the *y*-axis the title **Visitors**.

  f Do not display a legend.

  g Display the values (numbers) for each data point on the line.

  h Make sure that the chart is created on a full page on a sheet that is separate from the source data.

  i Set the *y*-axis range from **8300 to 9100**.

3 In the **footer**, enter your **name**, **centre number**, an **automatic date** and an **automatic filename**.

4 Save the file using the filename **artvisits**.

5 Print one copy of the line graph.

6 Close the file.

7 Check your printout for accuracy.

For this task, you will need the file **party** from the folder **files_graphs**.

Scenario

You work as a conference organiser. A national event has been organised to which representatives of the five main political parties have been invited.

1   Using suitable software for creating graphs, open the datafile **party** which contains data about the number of candidates representing the political parties.

2a Create a pie chart to show the **Representative** for each **Party**.

 b Title the chart **Political Party Representatives**.

 c Display a legend to identify the data.

 d Display the actual value (number, not percentages) for each sector.

 e Make sure that the chart is created on a full page on a sheet that is separate from the source data.

 f Make sure that the legend will clearly identify each sector on the printout.

3   In the **footer**, enter your **name**, **centre number**, an **automatic date** and an **automatic filename**.

4   Save the file using the filename **politics**.

5   Print one copy of the pie chart.

6   Close the file.

7   Check your printout for accuracy.

For this task, you will need the file **costs** from the folder **files_graphs**.

Scenario

You work in a housing development office. You have been asked to produce charts to display information for tenants.

1   Using suitable software for creating graphs, open the datafile **costs**, which shows the electricity costs for different apartment types.

2a Create a comparative bar chart to show the electricity costs for every **Season** for **Penthouse** and **Studio** apartments.

b   Display the **Season** along the *x*-axis.

c   Title the chart **Seasonal Electricity Costs**.

d   Give the *x*-axis the title **Season**.

e   Give the *y*-axis the title **Cost £**.

f   Use a legend to identify the bars. Make sure that the bars are distinctive and can be clearly identified when printed.

g   Display the values (numbers) for each bar.

h   Make sure that the chart is created on a full page on a sheet that is separate from the source data.

i   Set the *y*-axis range from **15 to 85**.

3   In the **header**, enter your **name**, **centre number**, an **automatic date** and an **automatic filename**.

4   Save the file using the filename **electric**.

5   Print one copy of the bar chart.

6   Close the file.

7   Check your printout for accuracy.

Task 1

Scenario

You are working in the London office of a company that employs sales people in various cities. The manager has asked you to create a spreadsheet to show the regional sales.

1 a Create a new spreadsheet.
  b Set the page orientation to **landscape**.

2 Enter the following data, leaving the **TOTAL** and **SALES** columns blank as shown.

REGIONAL SALES							
CITY	SEP	OCT	NOV	TOTAL	MINIMUM	WEIGHTING	SALES
LONDON	203	360	314		19	1.31	
BIRMINGHAM	231	369	538		22	1.49	
MANCHESTER	478	222	554		18	1.21	
CARDIFF	582	453	453		15	1.12	
NEWCASTLE	489	342	695		22	1.59	
CARLISLE	762	526	397		27	1.96	
OVERALL SALES							

You need to make some calculations in your spreadsheet.

3a In the **TOTAL** column use the **SUM** function to calculate the total for **LONDON** by adding the **SEP**, **OCT** and **NOV** figures.
  b Replicate (copy) this formula to show the **TOTAL** for all other cities.

4a Calculate the **SALES** for **LONDON** by multiplying the **TOTAL** by the **WEIGHTING**, then multiplying this figure by **1.15**.

(TOTAL*WEIGHTING)*1.15
  b Replicate (copy) this formula for the remaining cities.

5 In the **SALES** column, use the **SUM** function to calculate the **OVERALL SALES** figure. This is calculated by adding the **SALES** figures for all of the cities.

6a In the header enter your **name** and **centre number**.
  b In the footer insert an **automatic date** and an **automatic filename**.
  c Set the spreadsheet to fit on **one page**.

7 Make sure that all data is displayed in full.

8 Save the spreadsheet using the new filename **regsales**.

9 Print one copy of the spreadsheet on **one page** in **landscape** orientation, showing the figures, not the formulae.

Task 2

The manager has asked you to make some changes to the spreadsheet.

Open your saved spreadsheet **regsales**.

1a Delete the **MINIMUM** column and all its data.

  b Make sure blank cells do not remain where the data was deleted.

2a Insert a new column between **NOV** and **TOTAL**.

  b Enter data into the new column as shown below:

CITY	DEC
LONDON	450
BIRMINGHAM	430
MANCHESTER	400
CARDIFF	350
NEWCASTLE	450
CARLISLE	350

3 Make sure that the formulae in the **TOTAL** and **SALES** columns have updated after the DEC column was inserted.

4 Save your spreadsheet using the new filename **decsales**.

5 Apply the following alignments:

  a Centre the column label **REGIONAL SALES**.

  b **All** other text in the first column should be displayed as left-aligned.

  c Display all numeric data as right-aligned.

6 Format the numbers as follows:

  a Display the figures in the **TOTAL** column with a **currency symbol** and in **integer** format (zero decimal places).

  b Display the figures in the **WEIGHTING** column to **2** decimal places with no currency symbol.

  c Display the figures in the **SALES** column with a **currency symbol** and to **2** decimal places.

  d Display the figures in the other columns (SEP to DEC) in **integer** format (zero decimal places).

7 Add a **single outside border** beginning with the row label **OVERALL SALES** and ending with the **OVERALL SALES** figure in the **SALES** column.

8 Save the spreadsheet keeping the filename **decsales**.

Task 3

The manager would like you to make a few more amendments to the spreadsheet.

1 Make the following changes to the spreadsheet file **decsales**.

   a Change the NOV figure for LONDON to **814**.

   b Change the row label LONDON to **LONDON CITY**.

   c Change the WEIGHTING for BIRMINGHAM to **1.39**.

   d Make sure that the TOTAL and SALES figures have been updated as a result of these changes.

2a Save the spreadsheet keeping the filename **decsales**.

   b Make sure **gridlines** will be displayed on the printout.

   c Print one copy of the spreadsheet on **one page** in **landscape** orientation showing the **figures**, not the formulae.

3a Display the formulae. Make sure the formulae are displayed in full.

   b Make sure the page orientation is **landscape** and the spreadsheet fits on one page.

   c Make sure that **gridlines** and **row and column headings** (1, 2, 3, etc. and A, B, C, etc.) will be displayed when printed.

   d Save the spreadsheet formulae using the new filename **regform**.

   e Print the entire spreadsheet on **one page** in **landscape** orientation showing the **formulae**.

   f Make sure all formulae are displayed in full and are readable on your printout.

   g Close the file **regform**.

4 Close all open files.

For this task, you will need the file **grants** from the folder **files_graphs**.

Task 4

Scenario

The manager has asked you to produce a graph to show recent grant allocations.

1   Using suitable software for creating graphs, open the datafile **grants** which contains data on the grants given for the last six months.

2 a   Create a comparative line graph to show the grants given for **Medicine** and **Dentistry** from **April** to **September** inclusive.

   b   Display the months along the *x*-axis.

   c   Title the graph **Grant Allocations**.

   d   Give the *x*-axis the title **Month**.

   e   Give the *y*-axis the title **Number of Grants**.

   f   Use a legend to identify each line. Make sure that the lines and/or data points are distinctive and can be clearly identified when printed.

   g   Display the values (numbers) for each data point on both lines.

   h   Make sure that the chart is created on a full page on a sheet that is separate from the source data.

   i   Set the *y*-axis range from **10** to **45**.

3   In the **footer**, enter your **name**, **centre number**, an **automatic date** and an **automatic filename**.

4   Save the file using the filename **unigraph**.

5   Print one copy of the line graph.

6   Close the file.

7   Check your printout for accuracy.

The solutions for the Build-up tasks can be found in the folder **U2_workedcopies_buildtasks** on the **CD-ROM**. The solutions for the Practice tasks can be found in the folder **U2_workedcopies_practicetask** on the **CD-ROM**.

Preparation for the assessment

General assessment guidelines for all units

Before the assessment

Before you start a live assessment, complete at least two 'mock exams', e.g. OCR Sample Assignments in assessment conditions, without help from your tutor or classmates.

The assessment

- Level 1 assessments will usually be split into four tasks.
- You are allowed a notional duration of 2½ hours for each assessment.
- Before you begin, read through the paper to see what you will need to do.
- You may want to allow yourself about half an hour for each task and then half an hour to check all your final printouts and your saved files.
- Your tutor may allow you to complete an assessment over several consecutive sessions (lessons).
- Once you start an assessment your tutor cannot give you further teaching, and is not allowed to help you, so make sure that you are ready before starting a live assessment.
- Your tutor will provide you with a photocopy of the original assignment.
- Printing can be done after the assessment, however, you are advised to print your work whenever there is an instruction to print.

TIP!

When you have printed your work, do not move straight on to the next instruction or task! Check your printout against the instructions in the assignment to make absolutely sure that you have carried out each instruction correctly and that the printout matches what you have on the screen.

Headers and footers

Unless there is a specific instruction, you may use any font size, font type and alignment for headers and footers.

TIP!

Use the Tab key or the spacebar to insert spaces between header and footer items.

Your name

In many assignments you will be asked to enter your name, it is good practice to enter your first and last name.

Filenames

You are advised to enter filenames using the same case as in the assignment. However, you will not be penalised if you use different case for filenames. Do not enter a full stop after a file or folder name.

Computer-based assessment

If your work is going to be marked using computer-based assessment, then it is extremely important that you save all files in the correct folder and with the exact filename specified.

During the assessment

- During the assessment you are allowed to use:
  - the Heinemann textbook that you worked through for your learning
  - the Quick reference guides from the Heinemann textbook
  - your own notes
  - handouts from your tutor that cover general IT skills
  - any books that cover general IT skills.

- You are not allowed to use any books, notes, handouts, etc. that are referenced to the assessment objectives of the syllabus.

- You cannot ask your tutor or anyone else for help.

- If there is a technical problem e.g. something wrong with the computer or printer then you should inform your tutor or the invigilator.

- Read through the whole task before you start.

- All the instructions are numbered, and many have sub-steps (a, b, c, etc.). Read through the whole step before you start doing anything.

- Follow each instruction in the correct sequence. Do not leave out an instruction, even if you intend to do it later.

- Tick each instruction when you have completed it.

- Check that you have completed a step fully and correctly before moving on to the next step.

- Don't rush!

- Enter all data in the same case (i.e. capital/small letters) as in the assignment.

- Enter all data as it is presented in the assignment, ignore any alternative spelling suggestions made by the software.

- Any data that you have to type in is presented in bold to help you see what you have to key in. You should not use bold emphasis unless you are told to do so in the assessment.

- Make sure that the spell checker is switched on before you start and do a spell check again when you finish.

- Remember that if you find an error you can correct it, but if you leave the checking to your tutor, they cannot give your work back to you to correct any errors that they have found.

- If you notice an error, you can make changes to your work and print again.

- You can print as many draft copies as you wish, but you must remember to destroy any rough or incorrect copies.

- Where there is an instruction to enter your name, or to add your name to a file or folder name, then you must use your own first and last name, not the words 'Your Name'.

- You will be asked to enter your centre number, this can be done in any format: e.g. Centre Number 11111; Centre No 11111; Centre 11111; 11111.

TIP!

Read through all the instructions for the task before you start. If you are required to save the file with a different filename then do so **before** you start the task. This way you will not save over a file for the previous task.

At the end of the assessment

- Check your printout against the assessment paper. Use a different colour pen/pencil to tick each instruction on the copy of the assessment again.

- Make sure that you have saved all your files.

- Make sure that you have saved with the correct filename.

- Make sure that all your files are saved in the correct user area and/or folder.

- Make sure that every printout has your first and last name on it.

- Arrange your prints – put the final correct version of each printout in the order that they are listed in the assessment.

- Destroy any printouts that you do not wish to be marked (or hand these to your tutor making sure that your tutor knows these are not to be marked!).

- Hand to your tutor:
  - your final printouts in the correct order, you may wish to staple these to keep them secure
  - the copy of the assessment paper
  - the disk where you have saved your files (if you save on disk), if not tell the tutor where your files are saved on the computer.

Assessment guidelines for Unit 2

1 Your tutor will provide you with the file/s you need to create the graph(s) for the assessment.

2 Before an assessment you should create a new folder just for the assessment.

TIP!

Before you start, **COPY** the folder containing the file(s) into another user area in case you need to open an original file again.

Spreadsheet tasks

There will usually be three tasks covering spreadsheet skills.

- You will create a new spreadsheet, enter data and use formulae and functions.
- You will need to make some changes to your spreadsheet and save it with a different filename.
- You will need to format the updated spreadsheet and display the formulae.

Create a new spreadsheet

1 Make sure that you open a new spreadsheet, do not open an existing spreadsheet that may already have headers and footers or any data.

2 Set the orientation when instructed, do not leave it to be done later.

3 Do not enter the data in bold – it is presented in bold to help you to see what to enter.

4 You may use any font style or size unless otherwise instructed.

5 You will not be penalised if you leave a blank row below the spreadsheet title and/or below the column labels. However, you are advised not to leave a blank row below the column labels.

6 Double-check your work to make absolutely sure that you have entered all numbers with **100 per cent** accuracy.

7 If the instruction is to use a function you MUST use a function e.g. SUM, AVERAGE, etc. Do not use a formula even though this may also give a correct result.

8 Remember to read each instruction to calculate formula carefully. You may need to use brackets in a formula but you will not always be instructed to do so – you are expected to know when to use brackets.

9 Do not enter any additional data in any cells.

10 When asked to insert an automatic date and an automatic filename, do NOT type the date or the filename. You MUST use the automatic date and automatic filename option in Excel.

11 Always use **Print Preview**. Check that the data in all cells is fully displayed and that all headers and footers are correct.

Edit a spreadsheet

1 You will need to edit the spreadsheet that you created earlier.

2 Read through the task to see what the new filename should be.

3 Save your original spreadsheet with the new filename as soon as you open it. This will prevent you from saving over the original spreadsheet.

4 **Deleting a row/column.** You will need to delete either a row or a column.
- Make absolutely sure that you delete the whole row/column not just the data in the cells.
- Do not hide the row/column.
- The remaining rows/columns should 'close up' the gap.
- Check to make sure that the remaining rows/columns are automatically renumbered/relabelled.

5 **Inserting a row/column.** You will need to insert either a row or a column and enter data into the new row/column.
- Make sure that you insert the row/column in the correct position.

- Double-check to make sure all numbers that you enter are **100 per cent** accurate.
- Check to make sure that all formulae automatically recalculate.
- Refer to the printout of your original spreadsheet to check the original calculation results compared to the spreadsheet you are currently working on.

Format a spreadsheet

1 To display figures with a currency symbol, do not use the Currency icon on the toolbar. This displays as Accounting format which places the currency symbol (e.g. £ sign) to the far left of the cell and also moves figures further in from the far right of the cell.

2 When instructed to display gridlines, do not use the border option. Borders are not the same as gridlines. You will also be asked to use borders for selected cells, they should be darker than gridlines. For borders, choose the thick box border option as this will print more clearly.

3 When instructed to right-align numbers, even though they display as right-aligned, it is better to select the cells and the right-align icon (particularly important if your work is to be assessed electronically). The same applies to left and centre alignment of text.

4 Use Print Preview again to check that the data in all cells is fully displayed and that all headers and footers are correct (check for the updated filename).

Display formulae

1 Make sure that all columns containing formulae are wide enough to display formulae in full.

2 Make sure that you have used formulae where instructed. The value(s) must not be displayed in the cell(s).

3 Make sure that the source formulae have been copied where instructed. The formula in the rest of the row/column should be constructed in the same way (only the cell references should be different).

4 Formatting and alignment will not display on the formulae print; this is normal.

Graph task(s)

Create graphs

1 Use **Print Preview** before printing. After printing check your printout again. For any chart that displays a legend, make sure that the data is clearly distinctive

2 There will not be specific instructions about the points below but as good practice you should:
- remove the grey background from the plot area for bar charts and line graphs
- use a pattern fill for one or both sets of bars on comparative bar charts
- format lines to be thick and dark on line graphs
- use one dotted and one solid line for comparative line graphs
- set the print option to print in black and white to ensure that data is clearly distinctive for all graphs that display a legend (unless you have used pattern fills).

3 Charts with or without gridlines are acceptable.

4 Any intervals are acceptable on the y-axis, there is no need to change the default intervals set by Excel.

Good luck!

Index